You Mean I Have to Teach Science?

An Introduction to Teaching Elementary Science

Milt Huling. Ph.D.

Contributors: Tony De Souza, Ed.D., Arlene Fonda-Korr, Ed.D., Melissa Kelly, M.S. Ed., & Niqui Young Pringle Brown, M.Ed.

Candlelight Science
2022

Candlelight Science, LLC.
1025 S. Wilson
Bartow Florida 33830

email: mhuling1@outlook.com
website: candlelightscience.com

ISBN: 978-1-387-73646-1

Dedication

To my emotional support dogs (Joule, Midas, & Shadow), thank you.

Table of Contents

ABOUT THIS BOOK

The journey to write this book started as a solution to a multi-faceted problem. First, there is the issue facing many of our students that involve the high cost of textbooks, which places an unnecessary burden upon them. Second is finding a balance between the knowledge available to learn and the amount that can be learnt in any given time. Thirdly, I wanted to create a book that emphasized constructivism in a way to help new teachers visualize their role as an instructional facilitator. It is these three problems I hope to solve with this take on a science methods book designed specifically for beginning teachers and teacher candidates.

There is a push at many colleges and universities to reduce the costs for students when it comes to textbooks. In many cases, that is possible by using Open Educational Resources such as textbooks from sources like CK12.org or OpenStax. When it comes to straight content, these offerings are quite appropriate and have saved students hundreds of dollars in textbook fees. Unfortunately, there are no current OER science methods textbooks to choose from. To solve the cost issue, many science education professors have resorted to articles found online. While this can solve some problems in finding appropriately aligned content, it does not solve all of them. Many times, the articles are close, but not exactly what is wanted or needed to help teacher candidates gain better understandings of concepts, tasks, or methods.

Secondly, there are issues related to the voluminous nature of many textbooks marketed to beginning teachers and teacher candidates. The length of sections of these books tends to create a situation where students skim sections rather than truly read and reflect on them, even with accountability measures in place such as required quizzes and discussion posts. In order to help diminish this issue, I started to think about ways to alleviate this problem.

It is not that most currently available textbooks do not contain adequate information; they most certainly do. The accuracy, amount, and quality of content, in other books is not being challenged. The problem I see is that increases in number of words written on a topic does not always equate to increased knowledge retained by the reader, quite the opposite. But what if I incorporated recent changes in article lengths used by science journals currently marketed towards teachers? In recent months, article lengths have been reduced from 2,000 to 1,500 words maximum. If a shorter length is what works for their readers, should it not work equally well for our readers? At least that is the premise behind this work.

Third, by infusing constructivism, it is the hope new teachers can answer the question, “What is the role of the teacher in a reform-minded and academically successful classroom?” By definition, teaching is a profession that provides instruction, but what does providing instruction mean? How is providing instruction different from providing information? What does it look like in the classroom? It is the hope that as you read through this book, the reader will see and appreciate how a philosophy of teaching rooted in constructivism can help promote student academic success and achieve a more enjoyable classroom for all stakeholders.

The sections of this book have been used in my own state college classroom with much success. I also use them at a Tier 1 university where I work as an adjunct. The reflections based on the assigned readings are more concise and aligned to what I hope students are taking away from the reading. My hope is that you will have equal success.

ABOUT THE AUTHOR

Dr. Milt Huling received his Bachelor of Science degree in Earth Science from Southern Illinois University, his Master of Science degree in Science Education from Florida State University and his Ph.D. in Science Education from the University of South Florida. Milt has served in several leadership roles, having overseen both elementary and secondary science for a large district in the southeastern United States. Currently, Milt serves as the Professor of STEM Education at Polk State College in Lakeland, Florida. He also works as an adjunct at the University of South Florida and the University of Texas Rio Grande Valley teaching both masters and doctoral level courses.

Milt often refers to himself as a recovering high school physics teacher that has found his calling in the elementary science world. He now spends his days helping his teacher candidates learn to become transformational science teachers, as well as consulting for several educational technology companies. At night he spends time writing and creating curriculum for both math and science. To date, Milt has written over 400 science readers for grades K-8 and thousands of assessment items. You can see more of Milt's work at the following website: candlelightscience.com

More recently, Milt is working with a neuroscientist to help connect research in brain science with what is known from research about science education and literacy education. The goal is to find ways to assist teachers better reach struggling readers, namely those with dyslexia.

ABOUT THE CONTRIBUTORS

Dr. De Souza was previously with Polk County Public Schools and the Center for Guided Montessori Studies. He was formerly the Teacher Resource Specialist for the ESL program at the School Board of Polk County and served as the district's ESL teacher certification administrator. As a board member with the College of Education's Advisory Council at the University of South Florida, he assisted key district personnel from the school boards of Polk, Hardee, and Highlands counties with differentiated educational initiatives. Dr. De Souza was a council member on the Polk Vision Consortium for Post-Secondary Institutions and represented Southeastern University on that council when he was the Registrar at SEU. He is currently the Program Coordinator for the Educator Preparation Institute (EPI) and teaches in the education and business administration programs at Polk State College.

Dr. De Souza is originally from Hong Kong with more than 25 years of teaching and learning experience in higher education in Southeast Asia and the United States. Dr. De Souza holds a Bachelor of Arts in Elementary Education, a Master of Business Administration in Management Information Systems, and a doctorate in Education with a specialization in Applied Linguistics/ESOL. His research interests include the fundamentals of teaching English to speakers of other languages, preparing teachers for a career in education with children, and IT Management methods tied to the automation and support systems for decision making in a diverse cultural population.

Dr. Arlene Korr received her Bachelor of Arts degree in Elementary Education from Rider University, her Master of Arts degree in Special Education from Kent State University, her Education Leadership certification, and her Doctor of Education degree in Educational Leadership from the University of North Florida. These combined academic experiences have served Dr. Korr well in her roles as a classroom teacher, district administrator and assistant principal. During her 15-year tenure in public education, her focus had been on the creation of professional development strategies that enabled special education teachers to meet the instructional requirements of their diverse student population. Arlene's extensive experiences with best practice philosophies in support of adult learning provided her with an in-depth understanding of these challenges. To address these challenges, she integrated the essential resources into each training session to encourage successful teaching and learning.

Twenty-three years ago, Arlene's combined passion for curriculum and professional development led her to follow a career path in the world of education technology. During her time, "on the other side of the desk," she has traveled throughout Florida and meets with teachers, school leaders, school district leaders and the leaders from the Department of Education. She has attained this in her role as the account representative for education technology companies. During the past 18 years, Arlene's work has focused on the field of technology-based, science instructional resources. She enjoys working with teachers, school leaders and district leaders to develop unique professional development strategies to sustain the integration of technology to support inquiry-based science instruction. Arlene's primary effort has been to hear the voices of the science teachers and leaders and strongly consider the best available components for teachers to effectively teach science and to enable their students to develop a greater conceptual understanding of science.

Melissa Kelly has 30 years of experience in Elementary Education working with all grade levels. She received a Bachelor of Science degree in Elementary Education, as well as her Master's in Education with a Science, Technology, Engineering and Math focus at Warner University. Currently, she is working at Polk Avenue Elementary as the STEM lab teacher and Science Resource. The model she designed for her school is unique in that all 5th grade students come to her lab twice a week to participate in hands-on experiential learning activities. During this time, the student's classroom teacher stays in the lab to help facilitate the lessons as well as to gain the background knowledge necessary to integrate the day's science concepts back into their classroom lessons. Melissa also serves as an Adjunct Professor of STEM Education at Polk State College in Lakeland Florida. At Polk State College, Melissa teaches an Integrated Math, Science, and Technology course.

Niqui Young-Pringle-Brown was born and raised in Kingston, Jamaica. She currently resides in Lakeland, Florida with her husband and three sons.

Niqui received a graduate degree in education from the University of South Florida with a concentration in Reading. To put her newly minted credentials to use, she opted to leave the classroom and serve as a reading coach in a local elementary school. It was in this position that Niqui found her passion for helping underserved students achieve success in reading. Through her service with classroom teachers in a mentoring relationship, Niqui was able to attain success with her methodology for imparting to classroom teachers, strategies for teaching the major components of reading acquisition to children in K-5 classrooms. She has since used these skills to serve as a master presenter for Just Read, Florida, and The Annual Conference on the First Year Experience. Niqui continues to use the knowledge in her field to teach, coach, and mentor teacher candidates at Polk State College.

When she is not teaching and mentoring students, Niqui spends most of her time reading and traveling with her family and friends. She feeds her addiction to reading by reading at the beach on any given sunny afternoon.

INTRODUCTION

As you read this, maybe you are in your first years as a teacher, struggling like all of us have before you. Maybe you are just starting a teacher education program and are wondering what a day in the life of a science teacher should and can look like. To begin, let's step into the shoes of an expert elementary science teacher, Bindu. Bindu has been a teacher now for 7 years, so today is just another average day. By all measures, Bindu is a master science teacher, loved by her students and admired by her peers, but what traits does Bindu now possess that makes her so exceptional?

It's 7:00 am when Bindu pulls into the parking lot of the elementary school where she works. As she turns off her car, she runs through the checklist in her mind one more time to make sure she will be ready for her students to arrive at 8:05. She gathers her supplies she has packed into a grocery bag in the back of her car she bought from the store the week prior. As she walks toward the office entrance, she sees a few of her colleagues just pulling in. She gives them a quick wave and heads into the teacher workroom where she signs in for the day. Signing in is a common practice as it provides a list of who is on campus and to make sure all classrooms have coverage.

Once in her classroom, she turns on her computer and checks her email that may have come in since the night before. Occasionally, parents send her notes about students that may require her attention. From there she gives the room a quick check and begins to prepare the classroom for the days lessons by unpacking and organizing the supplies she brought, as well as gathering all the other items she needs from the equipment cabinet.

Today's lesson will cover the rates of dissolving. In this lesson, students will explore how different factors influence the rates of dissolving by using sugar cubes, which is one of the items Bindu purchased and brought in especially for this lesson. Bindu likes to have everything set up for students, so she prepares lunch trays with the equipment each group needs to conduct the investigation. She places spoons for stirring, beakers, stopwatches, and a data collection sheet for each student on each of the 6 trays. She then takes her two thermos containers down to the cafeteria. One container is filled with ice and water, which the other is filled with hot water. When she returns to the classroom, she fills a pitcher with room temperature water from the faucet in her room. She takes another look around her room before she sits down to double-check her lesson plan. As she looks over the lesson plan, she thinks about things like safety and student movements in the classroom during this lesson. She feels confident.

At 7:50 she takes a leisurely walk toward the lunchroom where she will collect her students. On the way she finds a minute here and there to say, “Hello,” to her friends. Before walking into the cafeteria, the principal stops her and asks how everything is going. Bindu shares her enthusiasm about today’s lesson and invites the principal to stop in. The principal excitedly agrees to do her best to come watch her young scientists in action.

Because of the masterful planning, Bindu’s classes runs smoothly, with each class completing the activity successfully. The principal did stop by and was pleased to see how well Bindu used questioning to promote student thinking as students explore the phenomenon, even congratulating her on the wonderful facilitation of the lesson.

As the last bus number is called and the last of the students leave the classroom, Bindu turns her attention to tomorrow. Again, she sits down and looks through the lesson plan to prepare. Tomorrow’s portion of the lesson involves graphing students collected data and then writing conclusions, so it will not require as many materials, but there are things that need to be in place before the morning.

Bindu finds the previously prepared PowerPoint that provides a quick overview of graphing for students that may need a little review. The example graph she is using has all the labels in English. She thinks about her two English Language Learner (ELL) students. She places another example graph next to the first with the labels translated into the student’s native language. Last year, she created picture cards with translations for this unit. Those are already displayed on her walls. She adds making another picture card for graphs to her ‘To Do’ list. That is something she can easily do and is vital for her ELLs understandings.

Bindu likes to provide her students with premade blank graphs that they cut out and glue in their science notebooks, so she will make a few copies before she leaves today. Each group will also be responsible for writing a conclusion based on their collected evidence. As Bindu has purposefully placed students in groups for this lesson she will not need to regroup them for this next task. During this portion of the lesson, Bindu plans to circulate around the room and give students only the amount of support they need, which will differ between groups and students. Once the groups are finished, they will present their data to the class along with their conclusions, demonstrating how scientists share their work.

It's the end of the day and Bindu heads back to the office where she will sign out and head for the parking lot. Tonight, is her son's soccer game. Fortunately, since Bindu is organized and well-prepared as a teacher, juggling work and family is not as difficult.

As you think about the day in the life of Bindu, it may seem easy as it is just organization. Unfortunately, it is much more. Throughout her teacher preparation program, she has learned many things that make her current masterful teaching possible, such as planning, classroom management, knowledge of exceptionalities, language barriers, lab safety, pedagogical knowledge, content knowledge, etc. It took Bindu several years to be able to seamlessly integrate all that she has learned into practice, which can be common, but now she feels confident about her practice and her success with her students is evidence of her mastery.

As you read the following chapters, think about how it applies to Bindu and her classroom. When did each play a role? How did she combine all this knowledge to create a seamless learning experience for her students?

CHAPTER 1: WHAT IS SCIENCE?

When you think about science, what comes to mind? Perhaps a better question, what do your current or future students think science is about? Do they recall their past experiences remembering reading a book filled with facts? Certainly, that is not the notion students should have about science. The goal is to have students feel like they are on an adventure or a journey into the unknown where they discover knowledge for themselves. While the previous sentences paint a mental picture of what a science classroom should look like, it still doesn't exactly explain science.

As it turns out, science is difficult to explain, and as a result, philosophers of science spend a great deal of their time contemplating the specifics of its composition, characteristics, and margins. What is certain is that science is a 'way of knowing' or making sense of the world. This way of knowing is governed by a set of tenants that guides and sets boundaries for the practice of science and even what can be considered scientific. These criteria, or boundaries, of science can be thought of, at least in part, as the following: repeatability, replicability, observability, naturally occurring, testability, falsifiability, and tentativeness.

Naturally Occurring
Observable
Testable
Repeatable
Replicable
Falsifiable
Based on Evidence
Tentative

Tenants of Scientific Practice

The reliability of scientific understandings depends on many factors. For example, science often searches for and analyzes trends to guide understandings. Looking at one piece of data may not tell the entire story about what is happening, or worse, can even cause misconceptions. The more times an experiment is conducted, the more information that will be provided. The more information (data) that is present, the more comfortable a scientist may be with regard to their claims based upon the information. It is the repeatability that allows for the establishment of faith in the scientific claim being made based on evidence.

Replicability enhances repeatability by having other scientists repeat the experiment or investigation in another location. To replicate something means to make another. In this case, replicable investigations mean a scientist can repeat an experiment somewhere else, or another scientist can conduct the same experiment as the first scientist. If an experiment can be replicated, it adds to the credibility of the original results. An experiment that works well in one location, but not in another could indicate a problem. If the results could not be replicated elsewhere, it may be because the results were not obtained based upon the original rationale. In science, it is important to be able to rule out variables in the natural world that scientists may not be able to control well, or possibly had not even considered.

Observability is another trait shared by science. Events or evidence of the event must be observed using the human senses (i.e., Taste, Touch, Sight, Hearing, & Smell). The scientists make observations by using their own senses or by using equipment to enhance or extend these senses. For example, humans do not have the ability to see an electron directly with our eyes, but the effects of an electron can be seen with the use of specialized equipment. The previous example is quite different from saying science can investigate something that cannot be seen. In the case of electrons, scientists can make observations through the extension of sight supplied by the special equipment.

The natural cause (mechanism) of the naturally occurring phenomenon must be testable, but also falsifiable. Through the process of science and the controlling of variables, experiments are performed to evaluate a claim. If science cannot perform a test to determine whether or not the claim is possible, then it cannot be considered scientific. If science does not have the tools to investigate unworldly, or other worldly causes, then science cannot be applied.

For example, a poor claim would be to investigate the existence of invisible swans. What if scientists looked for invisible swans and didn't find any, what would that tell us? It would not tell us they don't exist, but only they were not found. Therefore, it is not possible to reject the claim. If the claim being tested has no possibility of being rejected, it is not falsifiable. If it is not falsifiable, it cannot be scientifically tested.

Credit: Daniel Case Source: Wikimedia Commons License: CC BY-SA 3.0

Perhaps the most limiting factor of any scientific endeavor is that it is confined to the study of the natural world, hence the reliance on the tenants of naturally occurring and observable. Science is only capable of studying natural phenomena or processes that can be observed using the five senses or extensions of those senses through technology. Scientists may not use anything other than worldly phenomenon to explain an event. Evidence that entertains the possibility for a cause to be from aliens, ghosts, or astrology are not reasons that could be used to make a scientific claim. Just because an effect occurred that scientists cannot presently explain, the explanation of this observation could still be naturally occurring. By claiming an effect happened because of an unnatural (or paranormal) cause would be entering the world of pseudoscience.

Perhaps most important of all tenants of science is that science understandings are tentative. Unlike other disciplines, science expects that theories will eventually be revised with new evidence and new ways of looking at the evidence. As new evidence emerges, science understandings can either be modified to accommodate the added information or be replaced by a new theory that accommodates all current information. In contrast, theories can also change by looking at the same data in a new way. In this case, the viewpoint changes and not the data. Just like in other facets of life, different viewpoints can change your current understanding. As a result of either new data or changes in perspectives, theories will be changed or modified to accommodate these better understandings. It is also important to know that scientists use the terms ***support*** or ***reject.*** These terms are used to describe the outcome of an experiment. Scientists never use the term ***prove***.

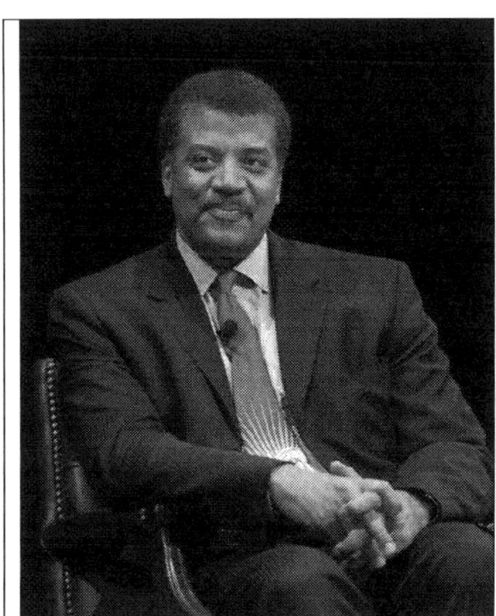

Credit: Bruce F Press Source: Wikimedia Commons License: CC BY 3.0

Conclusions

The definition of science is complicated just as science itself can be a complicated endeavor. In a nutshell, science has to do with asking questions about the natural world and making observations; but this description is overly simplistic and may provide more misconceptions than it provides answers. True, scientists make observation; but they do so in a certain way that sets it apart from other disciplines like history or art. These subtle differences between science and other disciplines are critical to obtaining an appropriate conception of science and are the focus of this text.

Simply put, it is a scientist's job to ask questions about and investigate the natural world. They are perhaps some of the most curious people in the world with their desire to obtain answers. It matters not where the questions lead the researcher. The variety of scientific investigations ranges from the depths of the oceans to the outer reaches of the universe. Whatever the focus of these investigations, all investigations look at some aspect of the natural world in an effort to create explanations of the mechanism to explain the phenomenon.

CHAPTER 2: TEACHING OF THE NATURE OF SCIENCE

The nature of science (NOS) is arguably the most important, but unfortunately the least known part of a science curriculum. In science classrooms, there is much time provided to the learning of what can be considered traditional content, such as the weather, properties of matter, interdependence amongst living organisms, etc. In contrast, NOS describes the characteristics of science knowledge, without which, science could not be distinguished clearly from other disciplines. For example, there are fields that share some of the attributes and even use some of the same tools as a scientist but are not science as defined by the tenants that guide the discipline of science. But what is the nature of science that K12 teachers need to cover to ensure our students become scientifically literate?

What Is the Nature of Science and Why Is It Important?

At present, there is a general consensus about the definition of NOS as it applies to science education in the K-12 setting. The current view of the nature of science can be thought of as how the scientific community passes judgment over what is accepted and what is not, or how much faith the community places on scientific knowledge (Marks & Eiks, 2009). To date, significant reform movements such as the National Science Education Standards (NRC, 1996), the Benchmarks for Scientific Literacy: Project 2061 (AAAS, 2009), NSTA position statement: Nature of Science (2000), the newly released Next Generation Science Standards (Achieve, Inc., 2013), plus the recent Perth Declaration (ICASE, 2007), emphasize the importance of the nature of science (NOS) as a key component to scientific literacy.

A benefit put forth for having an adequate understanding of NOS is that it enables the student to develop a better understanding of science content and provides them with the skills necessary to become a more informed decision-maker and better consumer of scientific information (McComas, Clough, Alamazroa, 1998). To help portray the importance of NOS on a global scale, this trend for increasing student understandings of NOS (as a part of scientific literacy) is not just limited to the United States (AAAS, 1990, 1993, 2009; Achieve, Inc. 2013; NRC, 1996; NSTA, 2000), but has pervaded reform movements globally (Matthews, 2009).

Currently, there is a set of characteristics that serve as a basis for most recent descriptions of NOS relevant to educational reform movements (Akerson et al., 2000); these include suggestions that scientific knowledge is:

- tentative (subject to change)
- empirically based (based on and/or derived from observations of the natural world)
- subjective (theory-laden)
- partly the product of human inference, imagination, and creativity (involves the invention of explanation)
- socially and culturally embedded
- distinguishing between observations and inferences
- promoting functions of and relationships between scientific theories and laws

Students often think that science is merely a set of facts that can be contained within textbooks. To understand NOS, students must come to grasp that science is a way of knowing, not what is known. Unlike other ways of knowing such as art, philosophy, religion, science is based on empirical research. By being empirical, science relies on observation and experimentation and not opinions or feelings. Even the language used in science is different than it is used outside of science, such as the term, "theory." For example, theories are not opinions. In the world of science, evidence precedes theories, not the other way around. Theories are also not insufficient forms of laws as one does not turn into the other, and they both can change with new evidence or new perspectives on the original evidence, which is a strength of science, not a weakness. Fortunately, the main tenants of NOS included in most state standards, but is that enough?

Despite the emphasis on NOS and its relevance within reform movements, success toward improvements in student understanding of NOS has been largely absent. Research has consistently shown that student's comprehension of NOS is not on a par with the contemporary vision of the science education community (Duschl, 1990; Lederman, 1992, 2007).

What Do We Know About Learning the Nature of Science?

In an extensive review of literature, Lederman (2007) explained that initial mid-century research painted a gloomy perspective of students' understandings of NOS. This initial research spawned an explosion of new curriculum in the 1960s and 1970s aimed at increasing the role of hands-on activities within science classrooms. Unfortunately, the enthusiasm about these new hands-on focused curriculum projects proved to be short-lived. Using the hands-on approach for students to perform the tasks of science in a procedural manner lacked the minds-on component called for in more recent reform movements (NRC, 1996). What is now called "cookbook" or procedure labs, placed a great emphasis on confirmation science. Attempts at using a historical perspective to improve students' understandings of the nature of science were also attempted with little to no success (Duschl, 1990). As Lederman et al. (2001) describe, neither method (implicit historical nor implicit using hands-on scientific inquiries) proved consistently successful at developing students' conceptions about NOS.

Fortunately, it was found that a manner of instruction using an explicit-reflective method did hold merit (Abd-El-Khalik et al., 1998; Abd-El-Khalik & Lederman 2000a; Akerson et al., 2000; Khishfe & Abd-El-Khalik, 2002). The explicit-reflective method provides a methodological approach to the instruction of NOS concepts that are planned for instead of wished for as some instructional side effect (Akindehin, 1988).

Clough (2007) suggests the effectiveness of an explicit-reflective approach should have come as little surprise. He suggests that inappropriate understandings of NOS, just like the more traditional misconceptions of content, are highly resistant to change. Implicit approaches in these cases would be ineffective at providing the necessary situations for conceptual change to occur. It makes little sense to believe that a highly resistant misconception of NOS would yield to a self-discovery method, just as it would for more traditional content. Furthermore, Lederman, Schwartz, Abd-El-Khalik, & Bell (2001) discussed how NOS should be taught in a manner similar to any other content specific knowledge where the teacher plans for and expects an outcome from instruction. Simply put, it should be planned for, taught, and assessed, and not just assumed it will occur as an artifact of instruction.

In defining explicit instruction, Abd-El-Khalik and Akerson (2009) point out that care must be taken, as explicit instruction can have varied meanings. Explicit does not mean "didactic," but rather planned for within a curriculum. The term "reflective" inherently includes complex ideas, theories, & principles when applied to instructional practice. Dewey (1933) defined reflection as a process requiring a learner to reconstruct and reorganize his understandings. In the view of Dewey, reflection is a rigorous process that is more disciplined than other types of thinking, such as: stream of consciousness, invention, and belief. According to Dewey (1916), as students are challenged by a state of disequilibrium, their own curiosity becomes the motivational impetus to satisfy their unsettledness. Reflection does not have a consistent methodology for implementation, but is more typically associated with student centered, inquiry based, active, or collaborative practices, all of which are considered constructivist methodologies.

Teacher Knowledge of NOS

Despite a half century of NOS being emphasized as part of reform movements, to this day teachers still have inadequate understanding of it (Clough, 2006). Science teachers tend to view science as value free and objective, devoid of uncertainty, and that any change from this focus on the facts of science (Larkin et al., 2009; Saka et al., 2009) would undermine this view.

A teacher's understanding of NOS is a necessary requirement, as teachers need to understand themselves what they are expected to teach. What is unfortunate is that teachers' conceptions of NOS are just as inadequate as students (e.g., Abd-El-Khalik & Lederman, 2000a; Duschl, 1990; Lederman, 1992, 2007; Schwartz & Lederman, 2002). For students to learn NOS, it would seem essential that teachers need to understand the humanistic manner of scientific work (Morrison, Raab, & Ingram, 2009).

Importance Teachers Place on NOS

What the science education community does know is that teachers make choices about what happens in their classrooms. These choices are based upon institutional factors such as school resources, goals, and culture. Institutional factors such as accountability are focused on short term student achievement that favors the adoption of a teacher-centered pedagogy that targets rote knowledge gains (Saka et al., 2009). To many, the goal of today's science learning is to prepare students for the next level of science with the emphasis of the facts of science (Larkin et al., 2009) and not the understandings by which science constructs its knowledge. The notion that the importance of science lies within the facts and process and not the nature of those understandings is at the heart of the problem. Lederman & Niess (1997) express the need for teachers to develop the attitude that NOS has equal or higher status than traditional content. Teachers must also develop the attitude that the knowledge of NOS will enhance students' understandings of more traditional science content. Teachers need to understand that the reform documents are not what makes the nature of science important, rather, it is included in reform documents because it is important.

Conclusions

Unfortunately, an all-too-common perception is that more traditional content is more critical to cover. To formalize what the science education community understands about the teaching and learning of NOS, two basic conditions must be met. First, teachers need to possess their own adequate understandings of NOS. Second, teachers must also develop the skills necessary to teach NOS through an explicit-reflective approach and must find the time to do so. With NOS a critical aspect of scientific literacy, it is vital to help students gain a better understanding of NOS if we want students to develop a deeper understanding of science and how its knowledge is developed.

References:

Abd-El-Khalik, F., & Akerson, V. (2004). Learning as conceptual change: Factors mediating the development of preservice elementary teachers' views of nature of science. *Science Education*, 88, 785-810.

Abd-El-Khalik, F., & Lederman, N. G. (2000a). Improving science teachers' conceptions of nature of science: A critical review of the literature. *International Journal of Science Education*, 22(7), 665–701.

Abd-El-Khalik, F., Bell, R. L., & Lederman, N. G. (1998). The nature of science and instructional practice: Making the unnatural natural. *Science Education*, 82(4), 417 – 436.

Achieve, Inc. (2013). *Next Generation Science Standards*. Achieve, Inc.

Akerson, V. L., Abd-El-Khalik, F., & Lederman, N. G.-b. (2000). The influence of a reflective activity-based approach on elementary teachers' conceptions of the nature of science. *Journal of Research in Science Teaching*, 37, 295–317.

Akindehin, F. (1998). Effect of an instructional package on preservice science teachers' understanding of the nature of science and acquisition of science-related attitudes. *Science Education*, 72, 73-82.

American Association for the Advancement of Science (AAAS). (1990). *Science for all Americans*. New York: Oxford University Press.

American Association for the Advancement of Science (AAAS). (1993). *Benchmarks for science literacy: A Project 2061 report.* New York: Oxford University Press.

American Association for the Advancement of Science (AAAS). (2009). *Benchmarks for scientific literacy* (revised). Retrieved September 20, 2010, from www.project2061.org/publications/bsl/online/index.php

American Association for the Advancement of Science (AAAS). (2009). *Benchmarks for scientific literacy* (revised). Retrieved September 20, 2010, from www.project2061.org/publications/bsl/online/index.php

Clough, M. P. (2006). Learners' responses to the demands of conceptual change: Considerations for effective nature of science instruction. *Science & Education*, 15(5), 463 – 494.

Clough, M. P. (2007). Teaching the Nature of Science to Secondary and Post-Secondary Students: Questions Rather Than Tenets. *The Pantaneto Forum*, 25. Retrieved from http://www.pantaneto.co.uk/issue25/front25.htm

Dewey, J. (1933). *How we think*. Buffalo, NY: Prometheus Books (Original work published 1910).

Dewey, J. (1966/1916). *Democracy and Education. An introduction to the philosophy of education* (1916 edn). New York: Free Press.

Duschl, R. A. (1990). *Restructuring science education*. New York: Teachers College Press.

International Council of Associations for Science Education. (2007). *The Perth Declaration on Science and Technology Education*. Perth, Australia: Australian Science Teachers Association (ASTA). Retrieved May 19, 2012, from http://www.icaseonline.net/perth.pdf

Khishfe, R., & Abd-El-Khalik, F. (2002). Influence of explicit and reflective versus implicit inquiry-oriented instruction on sixth graders' views of nature of science. *Journal of Research in Science Teaching*, 39(7), 551-578.

Larkin, D., Seyforth, S., & Lasky, H. (2009). Implementing and sustaining science curriculum reform: A study of leadership practices among teachers within a high school science department. *Journal Of Research In Science Teaching*, 46(7), 813–835.

Lederman, N. (1992). Students' and teachers' conceptions of the nature of science: A review of the research. *Journal of Research in Science Teaching*, 29, 331-359.

Lederman, N. (2007). The nature of science: Past, present, and future. In S. A. Lederman, *(Eds.), Handbook of Research on Science Education*. London: Lawrence Erlbaum & Associates.

Lederman, N., & Niess, M. (1997). The nature of science: Naturally? *School Science and Mathematics*, 97, 1-2.

Lederman, N., Schwartz, R., Abd-El-Khalik, F., & Bell, R. (2001). Preservice teachers' understanding and teaching of nature of science: An intervention study. *Canadian Journal of Science, Mathematics and Technology Education*, 1(2), 135 – 160.

Marks, R., & Eiks, I. (2009). Promoting scientific literacy using a socio-critical and problem-oriented approach to chemistry teaching: Concepts, examples, experiences. *International Journal of Environmental & Science Education*, 4(3), 231-245.

Matthews, M. R. (2009). Science, worldviews, and education. *Journal of Science and Education*, 18(6-7), 641-666.

McComas, W., Clough, M., & Alamazroa, J. (1998). The role and character of the nature of science in science education. *Science and Education*, 7, 511-532.

Morrison, J. A., Raab, F., & Ingram, D. (2009). Factors influencing elementary and secondary teachers' views on the nature of science. *Journal of Research in Science Teaching*, 46(4), 384-404. doi:10.1002/ tea.20252

National Research Council. (1996). *National science education standards*. Washington, DC: National Academy Press.

National Science Teachers Association. (2000). *NSTA position statement: Nature of science*. Retrieved February 9, 2010, from http:/ /www.nsta.org/about/positions/natureofscience.aspx

Saka, Y., Southerland, S., & Brooks, J. (2009). Becoming a member of a school community while working toward science education reform: Teacher induction from a cultural historical activity theory (CHAT) perspective. *Science Education*, 93, 996-1025.

Schwartz, R., & Lederman, N. (2002). "It's the nature of the beast": The influence of knowledge and intentions on learning and teaching nature of science. *Journal of Research in Science Teaching*, 39(3), 205 – 236.

CHAPTER 3: THE PRACTICE OF SCIENCE

As you are thinking about the practice of science, you may wonder, how is it different from the nature of science (NOS) previously discussed? What are the expectations for student knowledge within a typical curriculum? How does scientific practice that students do align with the practices that scientists do on a daily basis and why is it important for students to experience these practices?

As you may recall, the nature of science describes the characteristics of science knowledge, without which, science could not be distinguished clearly from many other disciplines. In contrast, scientific practices refer to the abilities needed to carry out science (NRC, 2012). While NOS and scientific practices are different, they are not mutually exclusive. Within the Framework for K-12 Science Education (Achieve, 2013), the claim is made that to fully understand both NOS and scientific practice, students must experience these scientific practices for themselves during authentic student-centered investigations.

The eight scientific practices offered by the National Research Council's (NRC) Science Framework for K-12 Science Education (Achieve, 2013) are:

- Asking questions
- Developing and using models
- Planning and carrying out investigations
- Analyzing and interpreting data
- Using mathematics and computational thinking
- Constructing explanations
- Engaging in argument from evidence
- Obtaining, evaluating, and communicating information

It is through these practices that trustworthiness of scientific work is established. It is also the expectation that scientists have integrity, collegiality, honesty, objectivity, and openness. To gain respect within the scientific community, scientists must be able to make systematic observations or experiments, identify variables, collect and organize data, interpret data in charts, tables, and graphics, analyze information, make predictions, and defend conclusions. The question that remains, how can we help students embrace and develop the habits of mind that are associated with these traits?

There has been a call for science education to be student-centered, content rich, and inquiry-based (NRC, 2001). It is important students develop the skills and abilities needed to perform scientific inquiry. To do so requires teachers to shift their role away from being the sole source of information to one of facilitator to help students learn the content using an inquiry-based approach (Olson & Loucks-Horsley, 2000). The previously cited research agrees with the NGSS protocols of how science should be taught (Achieve, 2013). By allowing students to participate in authentic science that mirrors the work of a scientist, allows students to make sense of the natural world, but what is at the heart of doing scientific practices?

Science has its roots in the acts of asking questions and making observations. Being able to think like a scientist requires students to have the opportunities to practice thinking like a scientist by asking and answering questions. Students will then use those questions to ask even more specific questions and then be able to turn those questions into a hypothesis which can then be tested either through an investigation or an experiment. From the data collected, we expect students to draw conclusions, share, and defend those results with their peers. If this sounds a lot like a science fair project, you are correct. In many states there are standards written to assess a student's practice of science knowledge that sound eerily like what is required of a student to participate in a science fair. While every student may not be required to compete in a science fair, it is the hope they develop the abilities within the classroom to be able to demonstrate those same skills to plan and carry out scientific investigations of various types (i.e., investigations or experiments); identify variables; collect and organize data; interpret data in charts, tables, and graphics; analyze information; make predictions; and defend conclusions.

In order or to achieve a level of trustworthiness of the findings of an experiment, a scientists must repeat their trials many times before they are shared with others. Even after the information is shared, it is retested by other scientists to validate the findings through a process known as **replication**. Only then, after much rigorous testing, does the new idea have a chance of being accepted by the larger scientific community.

A common misconception is that all science is derived from experiments. It is true, scientists do experiments where conditions are controlled, and variables are manipulated to learn about outcomes resulting from the manipulation. Within these experiments, scientists manipulate one variable at a time. This variable is called the independent variable. The variable that responds to these manipulations is called the dependent variable. While conducting these experiments, other potential variables are held constant, or controlled, to assure it is only the independent variable that is responsible for any resulting outcomes.

The DRY MIX mnemonic:
D - dependent,
R - responding,
Y - y-axis
M - manipulated
I - independent
X - x-axis

Sometimes it is not possible to do a controlled experiment, while other times it may not be desirable. A type of scientific study that does not control variables and looks for patterns in nature is called an investigation. Investigations are used when it is not possible to control variables, such as in the field of astronomy or weather. Other times, controlling variables may affect the behavior of what is being studied and are therefore best studied in their natural environment, such as wild animals.

Within the field of meteorology, it is not possible to control variables. Instead, meteorologists make painstaking observations of the weather around the world to better understand and predict future weather events. They use these observations to build models to help them better understand the world's weather. These models may be mathematical, visual, or conceptual. Scientists use models as tools when they are interested in studying an object or phenomena that are too complex, too remote, or too difficult to deal with as a whole. Models are a way to mimic the natural world to see patterns more easily. Most of Earth's systems are extremely complex and must be broken up into smaller and less complex parts for scientists to better understand these systems.

An individual scientific experiment or investigation may seem trivial in the bigger backdrop of scientific knowledge. In fact, it is those single bits of knowledge that builds the scientific knowledge that the world currently enjoys, but how does one investigation or experiment gain its way into this greater understanding of science?

Scientists share their findings and learn from each other's work in a process called, peer review. Scientists travel to conferences and present their work in front of their peers working in the same or similar fields. They also write up and publish their work in scientific journals. It is through this process, a single scientists work is reviewed and possibly replicated by other scientists who may eventually write up their own findings. Through this peer review process, the best ideas gain their way into the acceptance of the scientific community. Those ideas that do not enjoy the same positive response are discarded as a relic of the history of science. Whether the work of a scientist is accepted or not, all work is valuable in the creation of a stronger more resilient understanding of the natural world.

Because science involves doing many observations with much data, it can often be desirable to communicate this information visually. When done so, it is easier to identify and recognize patterns and correlations. Unfortunately, teachers often provide students the data tables or graphs, to analyze and interpret. This practice of providing tables and graphs often leaves students with an inability to create their own when called upon to do so. As part of the inquiry process, it is important for students to collect, record, graph, and analyze their own data. By doing so can help students better understand the relationships between independent and dependent variables in their investigation.

Research has demonstrated, that when students are authentically engaged in inquiry (i.e., the practice of science), both student engagement, as well as student achievement are increased (Lee & Songer, 2003). Research involving the 5E instructional model, a commonly used student-centered inquiry-based methodology, reveals how student achievement on standardized tests can almost double when implemented with only moderate fidelity (Coulson, 2002).

Given this evidence, clearly, a case can be made for allowing students the opportunities to conduct their own investigation or experiments, students learn the skills used by scientists. They also begin to learn how scientific knowledge is created. It is critical that for students to appreciate science and its practices, they must be provided ample opportunities to experience these scientific practices for themselves during authentic student-centered investigations.

References:

Achieve, Inc. (2013). *Next Generation Science Standards*. Achieve, Inc.

Coulson, D. (2002). *BSCS Science: An inquiry approach—2002 evaluation findings*. Arnold, MC: PS International.

Lee, H.S., & Songer., N.B. (2003). Making Authentic Science Accessible to Students. *International Journal of Science Education.* 25(1), 1-26.

National Research Council. (1996). *National science education standards*. Washington, DC: National Academy Press.

National Research Council. (2012). *A Framework for K-12 Science Education: Practices, Crosscutting Concepts, and Core Ideas*. Washington, DC: The National Academy Press.

Olson, S., & dan Loucks-Horsley, S. (2000). *Inquiry and the National Science Education Standards: A Guide for Teaching and Learning*. Washington DC: National Academic Press. https://doi.org/10.17226/9596

CHAPTER 4: LAB SAFETY

You have probably heard the saying, “Safety First.” In a science classroom, this statement applies even more for the teacher than the participating student. As a teacher of science, it is understood there is potential danger given the hands-on activities, but fear of accidents should not limit hands-on science. Safety in the science classroom is about a teacher’s knowledge, preparation, and knowing what to do in case of an accident.

As a caveat, this section is provided to provoke awareness of lab safety, not to provide an exhaustive dissertation about all aspects of lab safety. Within this section you will see links provided to other resources to find specific grade level information. The hope is to provide the teacher candidate or new teacher with an overview, helpful tips, and a calming voice. With knowledge, the fear of lab safety can be diminished.

Science teachers owe their students a duty of care to anticipate and mediate (prevent) potential dangers that may be imposed in the science classroom. Failing to do so is considered negligence by not protecting students from unreasonable risk. Failure to provide such duty of care can result in a loss of a state teaching license or even worse. This duty of care also extends to projects or assignments that are caried out by students at home.

As you prepare to do hands-on investigations in your science classroom, it is important to document all safety procedures and safety warnings that are explicitly issued to students prior to each investigation. One straightforward way to do this is to have the safety protocols listed on the lesson plans. This documentation of protocols can then be a reminder of what to mention to students before the start of the investigation. Another great option is to list safety protocols as part of any written instructions provided to students. For example, there may be highlighted notes reminding students to always wear safety glasses. Not only does this method help everyone to know what is required to be safe, it is also the critical documentation that can be used as evidence of Duty of Care (Stroud & Roy, 2015) should an accident occur.

One of the first tasks to prepare for safety in the classroom is to make students aware of their role in lab safety by establishing rules. These rules should be established on day one of your course. Most school districts will have a safety protocol in place. These protocols may be passed down to the school level via a science lead. When in doubt about established rules by institutions such as districts or schools, ask.

For example, a district may have a set of common rules that are to be gone over with students before any hands-on investigation are to be done. To ensure these rules have been understood by the students, most districts have a lab safety document, typically requiring the signature of both the student and parent. An example of a lab safety contract can be obtained from the National Science Teacher Association website at the following links:

- **Elementary**: (https://static.nsta.org/pdfs/SafetyAcknowledgmentForm-ElementarySchool.pdf)

- **Middle School**: (https://static.nsta.org/pdfs/SafetyAcknowledgmentForm-MiddleSchool.pdf)

- **High School:** (https://static.nsta.org/pdfs/SafetyAcknowledgmentForm-HighSchool.pdf)

Again, your school or district may have a version like this that is aligned to the specific needs of different grade levels. Signed lab safety contracts are to keep both students from harm and to help protect the teacher from liability in case an accident does occur.

It is also highly recommended secondary science teachers take the 7-hour online training course through the Flinn Scientific website which can be found at the following link: https://www.flinnsci.com/online-resources/lab-safety-courses/

The Flinn online safety course reports to cover every aspect of science lab safety, including right-to-know laws, SDS requirements, the proper use of personal protective equipment, and safe laboratory practices. For elementary science teachers, it would be useful to study the following document from the National Association of Science Teachers entitled *Safety in the Elementary Classroom* (NSTA, n.d.): https://static.nsta.org/pdfs/SafetyInElementaryScience.pdf

Fortunately, there are simple ways to protect yourself from financial harm and your students from physical harm. Many safety rules that need to be in place in a science classroom are common sense rules related to student behavior. Therefore, safety instructions must always include behavior expectations of students, such as:

- Follow the teacher's directions.
- Always check with the teacher before conducting activities.
- Report all spills, glass breakage. etc.
- Always wear proper clothing.
- Do not eat or drink in the laboratory area.
- Keep the work area clean.
- No horseplay.

Science classrooms, even more so than other classrooms, need to be orderly as this provides the safest environment for students. Teachers need to be clear how students will obtain materials or have a plan for how materials will be distributed. A disorganized science classroom is not a safe classroom (Kwan & Texley, 2002). As elementary classrooms, and even many middle school classrooms may not be arranged to allow easy access for cleanup or retrieval of supplies, identifying roles for each team member is important to avoid excessive student movement. Lab safety also extends to post-investigation activities such as proper clean up and hand washing. These activities too may need to be choreographed to reduce student movement.

Teachers also need to look at all hands-on investigations with a critical eye and ask themselves, is there a safer way? For example, do younger students need to use an electric burner to heat water in preparation for an investigation of temperature versus rates of dissolving? Using the electronic burner exposes students to the potential risk of being burned or exposed to electric shock. As an alternative, especially for younger students, all that is necessary for this investigation is water of different temperatures. A safer alternative might be to have warm water (either preheated in a thermos or just hot water from a tap), room temperature, and cold water readied with the use of ice cubes kept safely in a thermos.

While most investigations carried out in an elementary science classroom are done with household chemicals, such as vinegar, baking soda, corn starch, calcium chloride, sodium chloride (table salt), etc., it does not mean these chemicals are necessarily safe. All chemicals, whether common household chemicals or not, should be kept in a drawer, cabinet, or closet and always behind lock and key, being clearly marked as chemical storage.

Verbally restricting students from an area is not sufficient. It may be viewed as creating an attractive nuisance and not exercising an appropriate duty of care. A science teacher must also have on file the "Materials" Safety Data Sheet (SDS) sheets for each chemical you have in your classroom as these contain valuable information. The following link provides additional information regarding SDS:
https://www.osha.gov/sites/default/files/publications/OSHA3514.pdf

These Safety Data Sheets should be kept in a notebook near the cabinet or room/closet where chemicals are stored. It may also be a good habit to have these attached to your lesson plans that are kept on file electronically. Again, check with your district about their required protocols.

One significant difference between an elementary and secondary classroom is that glassware should be replaced with plasticware in an elementary classroom. This can minimize the danger of cuts by students who may still be developing their fine-motor skills. Make sure students understand plasticware or glassware is used only for investigations and is not to be used for other purposes, such as drinking.

When students are conducting investigations where substances that may be splashed into eyes proper protective eyewear should be always worn. This also goes for any investigation involving either actual or potential projectiles. American National Standards Institute (ANSI) code Z87 or Z87.1 has provided guidance on the types of chemical splash goggles (only types G, H, or K) that are approved. These are available in small sizes to fit elementary students. After each use, protective eyewear should be disinfected using alcohol wipes making sure to clean the both the eyewear and strap. There are disinfecting cabinets that use ultraviolet light, but are common only in secondary science classrooms.

Elementary science classrooms should have minimal, but not zero risk. By understanding your duty of care, you can choose appropriate lessons, establish safe classroom practices, and provide students with knowledge of how to be safe. By being knowledgeable, careful, and strategic you can provide a safe environment for students to learn about science using the hands-on methods that are critical to building sophisticated understandings of science concepts.

References:

Flinn Scientific (n.d.). Lab Safety Courses. Retrieved 6/14/2022 @ https://www.flinnsci.com/online-resources/lab-safety-courses/

Kwan, T., & Texley, J. (2002). *Exploring Safely: A Guide for Elementary Teachers*. Arlington, VA: NSTA Press. https://portal.ct.gov/-/media/SDE/Science/Safety/scisaf_cal.pdf

National Science Teacher Association (n.d). *Safety In Elementary Science.* Retrieved 10/19/2021 @ https://static.nsta.org/pdfs/SafetyInElementaryScience.pdf

National Science Teacher Association (n.d.). Elementary Science Safety Acknowledgment Form. Retrieved 6/14/2022 @ https://static.nsta.org/pdfs/SafetyAcknowledgmentForm-ElementarySchool.pdf

National Science Teacher Association (n.d.). High School Safety Acknowledgment Form. Retrieved 6/14/2022 @ https://static.nsta.org/pdfs/SafetyAcknowledgmentForm-HighSchool.pdf

National Science Teacher Association (n.d.). Middle School Safety Acknowledgment Form. Retrieved 6/14/2022 @ https://static.nsta.org/pdfs/SafetyAcknowledgmentForm-MiddleSchool.pdf

Occupational and Health Administration (n.d.). Hazard Communication Standard: Safety Data Sheets. Retrieved 6/14/2022 @ https://www.osha.gov/sites/default/files/publications/OSHA3514.pdf

Stroud, L., & Roy, K. (2015). *Science Laboratory Safety Manual* (Third ed.). Raleigh, NC: Science & Safety Consulting Services.

CHAPTER 5: MANAGING THE SCIENCE CLASSROOM

Will you be prepared for your first day in your own science classroom? At this point, you have proven your content and teacher professional knowledge on state exams, and even received a diploma which verifies you are believed to have the ability to teach science. You prepared all summer by looking at the course description, reviewing standards that need to be covered, and thinking about how to set up your room. You have compiled lesson plans to cover every aspect of content, so what is left to do and why do you still feel unprepared? Is it because up until now your preparation was about you being ready and not what your students need? Being in a new classroom with new students, a teacher needs to be able to direct students in a way that best accommodates their learning needs, so what needs to be adjusted in a classroom environment for students to feel successful?

Establishing Classroom Norms and Expectations

Perhaps not surprising, the expectations you set in the classroom are correlated to student behavior. Simply put, for students to be successful at achieving your expectations, they must know what they are and how they can be successful in meeting them (Brophy, 1998; Evertson, Emmer, & Worsham, 2003; Evertson & Harris, 1992). It is critical that a teacher establishes expectations early as student require realistic, academic, and behavioral expectations (Brophy, 1998). This early expectation setting with the addition of ongoing reminders and consistent enforcement will go a long way towards improving your student's academic achievement and engagement during activities (Evertson, 1985; 1989; Evertson & Emmer, 1982; Evertson, Emmer, Sanford, & Clements, 1983; Johnson, Stoner, & Green, 1996). In fact, students favor classrooms where teachers exert authority and hold them to higher standards (Good & Brophy, 2000). These higher standards, or expectation that are set, especially in the early grades can have far reaching consequences on a student future performance (Wong & Wong, 1998).

Turning Expectations into Rules

Whether it is during instruction or just overall classroom environment, students need structure. If there is structure to instruction, students learn by practice. In classrooms where clear and concise rules are established, students can more easily conform to them by knowing where the boundaries of behavior start and end. This includes how students speak to one another, to the teacher, as well as the respect shown to students when the teacher speaks to them.

When speaking to students whether it be for praise or behavior correction, it is important to always communicate care and respect for the students. How a teacher responds to a students' actions and interactions will go a long way in helping a student become a more responsible and self-regulated learner (Brophy, 1998). By providing classroom rules, a teacher sets the tone for the classroom environment in ways far beyond student behavior as they can also be inferred by a student that the teacher cares for their well-being as both a person and a student (Brophy, 1998). So, how many rules are needed to attain the desired learning environment and who sets them?

The number of rules you choose and even which you choose is a matter of choice, but certainly, research tells us that fewer rules are better than an exhaustive list. A way to accomplish this is by keeping the number small, have no exceptions, and apply to everyone in the classroom, to include the teacher. What research tells us is that having students help to set the rules provides them with ownership (Castle & Rogers, 1993; Martin & Hayes, 1998) and provides a means for making them understandable by all. It is also important to choose the phrasing of rules, so they demonstrate the positive rather than what not to do. For example, raise your hand before speaking versus NO BLURTING OUT.

Procedures on the other hand may be more numerous than rules and be more specific to certain tasks, but like rules, they must be understandable to all parties (Evertson & Harris, 2003). Procedures may include the more process-oriented tasks that occur in your classroom, such as acquiring permission to use the washroom, get a drink, or sharpen a pencil. There may be specific procedures for when students are conducting inquiry labs, such as safety precautions, group roles, special movement restrictions in the lab settings. Other procedures might be to check the board when entering the classroom for directions, such as get out your science notebook, answer the question on the board, etc.

Pedagogy as a Management Tool

When was the last time you sat through an hour or more of lecture? Imagine how you felt not feeling engaged by the lesson, now imagine a child with far less self-control. An exciting, dynamic, and fast-moving classroom can be a meaningful change when you are struggling with behavior issues. All the rules and procedures cannot overcome what happens when a student is not engaged with the learning and becomes bored.

Mix up instruction by using a variety of tasks and learning styles. Even a great system can get boring over time. If, after every hands-on activity you have students write a reflection or summary, try adding some spice by having students create wanted posters or other infographic, or create a rap to explain the concept being learned. Consider starting lessons with a discrepant event of a socioscientific issue to promote interest. By utilizing a mixture of approaches to both pedagogy and learning styles, engagement and excitement increases while behavioral issues decrease (Young & Roberts, 2013).

Interpersonal Interactions in Student-Teacher Relationships

It comes as little surprise that research supports the notion that teachers have a positive impact in shaping students' relationship with school in general. This student-teacher relationship plays a crucial role in increasing student engagement (Groves et al., 2015). Developing this student- teacher relationship is perhaps the first and most crucial step in helping students become academically successful by creating a learning environment that is both motivating and engaging (Dotterer and Lowe, 2011). Such an environment can also provide other positive outcomes such as classroom behavior, support overall adjustment to school, improvements in social skills and promote academic performance (Battistich, Schaps, & Wilson, 2004; Birch & Ladd, 1997; Curby, Rimm-Kaufman, & Ponitz, 2009; Ewing & Taylor, 2009; Hamre & Pianta, 2001; Rudasill, Reio, Stipanovic, & Taylor, 2010). Students who had a close inter-personal relationship established with their teacher were less likely to miss school, more independent in their learning, more willing participants in classwork, and overall, more engaged in their learning (Birch & Ladd, 1997; Decker, Dona, & Christenson, 2007; Klem & Connell, 2004). Positive relationships with students combined with a learner-centered (such as a constructivist inquiry-based science classroom) can also increase motivation in students when compared to teacher-centered classroom (Daniels & Perry, 2003).

Conclusions

In the classroom, preparation and success go hand in hand. This can be no truer than preparing to manage your own classroom. Classroom management covers many aspects and is essential for the academic success of students. Your rules (developed preferably with your students) should support your learning goals for the class by providing an environment conducive for learning. The rules you develop should be easy to follow making students feel successful and be clear about consequences, both positive and negative. Beyond having rules and procedures, it is also vital that you as a teacher make the time to develop relationships with students to enhance their success in both academic achievement and behavior in general. While rules and procedures may vary by content, grade level, etc. boundaries, structure, and a caring teacher can go a long way to providing everything a teacher needs to have a successful year.

References:

Battistich, V., Schaps, E., & Wilson, N. (2004). Effects of an elementary school intervention on students' "connectedness" to school and social adjustment during middle school. *The Journal of Primary Prevention,* 24(3), 243-262.

Birch, S. H., & Ladd, G. W. (1997). The teacher-child relationship and early school adjustment. *Journal of School Psychology, 55*(1), 61-79.

Brophy, J. E. (1998). Motivating students to learn. Boston: McGraw-Hill.

Castle, K., & Rogers, K. (1993). Rule-creating in a constructivist classroom community. Childhood Education, 70(2), 77–80.

Curby, T. W., Rimm-Kaufman, S. E., & Ponitz, C. C. (2009). Teacher-child interactions and children's achievement trajectories across kindergarten and first grade. *Journal of Educational Psychology,101* (4), 912-925.

Daniels, D. H., & Perry, K. E. (2003). "Learner-centered" according to children. Theory Into Practice, 42(2), 102-108.

Decker, D. M., Dona, D. P., & Christenson, S. L. (2007). Behaviorally at-risk African American students: The importance of student-teacher relationships for student outcomes. *Journal of School Psychology, 45*(1), 83-109.

Dotterer, A. M., and Lowe, K. (2011). Classroom context, school engagement, and academic achievement in early adolescence. *J. Youth Adolescent.* 40, 1649–1660. doi: 10.1007/s10964-011-9647-5

Evertson, C. M. & Emmer, E. (1982). Effective management at the beginning of the school year in junior high classes. Journal of Educational Psychology, 74, 485–498.

Evertson, C. M. (1985). Training teachers in classroom management: An experiment in secondary classrooms. Journal of Educational Research, 79, 51–58.

Evertson, C. M. (1989) Improving elementary classroom management: A school-based training program for beginning the year. Journal of Educational Research, 83(2), 82–90.

Evertson, C. M., & Emmer, E. T. (1982). Effective management at the beginning of the school year in junior high classes. Journal of Educational Psychology, 74, 485–498.

Evertson, C. M., & Emmer, E. T., Sanford, J. P., & Clements, B. S. (1983). Improving classroom management: An experiment in elementary classrooms. The Elementary School Journal, 84, 173–188.

Evertson, C. M., & Harris, A. H. (2003). COMP: Creating conditions for learning. Nashville, TN: Vanderbilt University.

Ewing, A. R., & Taylor, A. R. (2009). The role of child gender and ethnicity in teacher-child relationship quality and children's behavioral adjustment in preschool. *Early Childhood Research Quarterly, 24*(1), 92-105.

Good, T. L., & Brophy, J. E. (2000). Looking in classrooms (8th ed.). New York: Longman.

Groves, M., Sellars, C., Smith, J., and Barber, A. (2015). Factors affecting student engagement: a case study examining two cohorts of students attending a post -1992 university in the United Kingdom. *Int. J. High. Educ.* 4, 27–37. doi: 10.5430/ijhe.v4np27

Hamre, B. K., & Pianta, R. C. (2001). Early teacher-child relationships and the trajectory of children's school outcomes through eighth grade. *Child Development*, 72, 625-638.

Johnson, T. C., Stoner, G., & Green, S. K. (1996). Demonstrating the experimenting society model with classwide behavior management interventions. School Psychology Review, 25(2), 199– 214.

Klem, A. M., & Connell, J. P. (2004). Relationships matter: Linking teacher support to student engagement and achievement. *Journal of School Health*, 74(7), 262-273.

Martin, H., & Hayes, S. (1998). Overcoming obstacles: Approaches to dealing with problem pupils. British Journal of Special Education, 25(3), 135–139.

Rudasill, K. M., Rimm-Kaufman, S. E., Justice, L. M., & Pence, K. (2006). Temperament and language skills as predictors of teacher-child relationship quality in preschool. *Early Education and Development*, 17(2), 271-291.

Young, S., and Roberts, M. (2013) *The New Science Teacher's Handbook*. National Science Teacher Association Press.

Wong, H.K. and Wong, R.T. (1998). The First Days of School. Mountain View, CA: Harry K. Wong Publications, Inc.

CHAPTER 6: SCIENTIFIC INQUIRY AND ITS USE IN THE CLASSROOM

Most of us have had experiences with science being textbook driven, where students learn facts from lecture or reading. This practice of learning science as a predetermined collection of facts is far too common within the American Education system, despite the best efforts of reformers. A question that must be asked is, "What is the goal or purpose of teaching science in a K12 venue?" Is it to create students with knowledge of scientific factoids and vocabulary terms from a textbook? If so, how does a student discern the difference between other human endeavors, such as history, literature, music, or art? Perhaps this notion of the purpose of science would be enough if the end goal were to send our students on to win game shows, but hopefully we want more, where knowledge of facts without understanding has limited merit.

Scientific literacy is recognized globally as a method of increasing both the economic and industrial advancement of nations. We also need every citizen of the world to be critical consumers of information in a world steeped in science and technological issues (Fensham, 2008). To meet the first goal requires a concerted effort to establish a means to identify and train the next generation of scientists. It will be this next generation that will have an impact on the economics of the nation and improve the personal health of its citizens (Huling, 2015). Simultaneously, it is equally important that those not considering science as a vocational pathway also become scientifically literate to support a more sustainable vision of growth (2008). As we now live in an inter-connected world as revealed by global pandemics, pollution, land-use, and even global supply chain issues, each member of society will make choices about the collective vision of science through the spending of their money or via the ballot box where they choose which programs to support.

The question remains, what does the science classroom need to include to achieve these goals? Do we want our students to have a sophisticated understanding of how scientific knowledge is created and how that knowledge is different from other ways of knowing? Do we want students to understand that the process of inquiry is how scientific knowledge is constructed? If so, then it requires the teaching of science as inquiry and not rote learning of facts and vocabulary, but what is inquiry?

> *"Scientific inquiry refers to the diverse ways in which scientists study the natural world and propose explanations based on the evidence derived from their work. Inquiry also refers to the activities of students in which they develop knowledge and understanding of scientific ideas, as well as an understanding of how scientists study the natural world. (National Science Education Standards, 1996, p. 23."*

Unfortunately, even this definition by the National Research Council leaves much room for ambiguity. Some teachers regard any instruction that is hands-on and active to be inquiry-based (Bonwell & Eison, 1991). Other teachers perceive inquiry as something beyond just hands-on instruction, where students take on a role much like a scientist by generating their own questions, designing their own investigation, conducting the investigation, making their own conclusion based on the collected information, and in the process, discovering next steps to be taken for further inquiries (Krajcik et al. 2000). Is it any wonder why teachers struggle with doing inquiry when they may lack a proper understanding of what is inquiry?

One such way of simplifying inquiry is by looking at the levels of inquiry. In the classroom, inquiry has multiple levels, perhaps most clearly defined by Schwab (1962) and Herron (1971). Variations have found their way into modern publications more recently (Bianchi & Bell, 2008). They are commonly referred to as the 4 levels of inquiry.

1. <u>Confirmation inquiry</u>: students are provided with the question and procedure and the known outcome. Confirmation science is often referred to as cookbook science for obvious reasons.
2. <u>Structured inquiry</u>: students are provided with the question and procedure, but not the outcome. Students are asked to generate an explanation supported by the collected data. Structured inquiry is perhaps the most common of all levels.
3. <u>Guided inquiry</u>: students are provided with the research question. The students are expected to develop procedures for the collection of data and develop an explanation based on the findings. Many states have standards that require students to be able to design their own experiment or investigation.
4. <u>Open inquiry</u>: students develop their own questions, design, and carry out investigations, as well as communicate their results. Open inquiry is the type of inquiry used in science fair competitions.

Figure 1. Levels of Inquiry and Information Provided by Teacher

Level of Inquiry	Question Provided	Procedure Provided	Solution Provided
1 Confirmation inquiry	X	X	X
2 Structured inquiry	X	X	
3 Guided inquiry	X		
4 Open inquiry			

While all levels of inquiry have their place, the goal is to match what needs to be learned with the experience your students have with doing inquiry. Both confirmation and structured inquiry can be used in both upper and lower elementary grades to either acquaint or reacquaint students with the skills of inquiry, such as, practicing a specific inquiry skill, or collecting and recording data (Bianchi & Bell, 2008). In upper grades, confirmation or structured inquiry can be used to reinforce previously learned materials and act as a launching pad to move a lesson into a higher level of inquiry. For example, a lesson may start with collecting data to confirm an idea, after which subsequent trials can be conducted by having the teacher choose another variable to test and leaving the conclusion making to the students or even having students design the inquiry themselves to test the teacher's question. If students are ready, they can be asked if they have a question that can be investigated, moving the investigation to an even higher level of inquiry.

It is important to note, that at the Guided and Open levels of inquiry does not mean the students are in full control of the experiment. It is strongly recommended that all aspects of the investigation are developed through consensus with the teacher, ensuring the target learning is guaranteed and a safe environment is maintained.

Teaching science through Inquiry has become synonymous with good instruction. "Science is something students do, not something that is done to them" NRC, 2000). For example, students do not come to understand inquiry by rote memorization of terms or steps used in the methods of science. For students to understand how scientific knowledge is created through inquiry, students need to do inquiry in a hands-on minds-on manner.

The explanation above describes why teaching through inquiry, but it is not always easy given that most classroom teachers do not have expertise in the inquiry process used by a professional scientist. Some teachers are even resistant (see section on epistemological beliefs and practice). Teachers are often heard making statements of how they are old school, perhaps to cover their disapproval or maybe fear of using inquiry as a form of instruction in their classroom. In fact, the roots of inquiry can be traced back to Dewey (Bybee and DeBoer, 1993; DeBoer, 1991) who contended that science should not be taught as a collection of facts and should instead have a focus on "science as a way of thinking and an attitude of mind" (Dewey, 1910, p.70), which sounds very much like the hands-on minds-on approach called for in recent reform movements (NRC, 1996). Dewey also thought students should learn the process of sciences or methods of science (Dewey, 1910). "If students need to learn the methods of science, then how better to learn than through active engagement in the process of inquiry?" (NRC, 2000). By the 1950s and 60s the rationale for such instruction became clear. So, when a teacher proclaims to be "old school" and not in favor of inquiry one must wonder, how old would that make them? Is this comment masking an even more deeply rooted issue pertaining to how they view knowledge and knowledge construction? In cases where this occurs, cookbook science or just teacher demonstrations are commonly used by teachers who struggle to give up control of the learning.

Beyond the reluctance to change their practice, there are also other barriers that prevent the utilization of inquiry for even the more willing. As described by Fitzgerald, Danaia, & McKinnon, (2019), these common barriers include "extreme time restrictions on all scales, the poverty of their common professional development experiences, their lack of good models and definitions for what inquiry-based teaching actually is, and the lack of useful resources enabling the capacity for change."

The National Science Education Standards (NRC, 1996) explains that the teaching of science requires students to have more than just the knowledge of scientific information, it also necessitates students to learn, by participation, about the skills of inquiry and how the process of inquiry explains how scientific knowledge is created. Students cannot learn about inquiry by learning only its vocabulary such as "hypothesis" and "inference" or the procedural steps used in scientific investigations. To truly gain an understanding of science, students must participate directly in the endeavor of inquiry to develop the sophisticated understandings that will help us meet our goals to have a scientifically literate citizenry.

References:

Bianchi, H., & Bell, R. (2008). The Many Levels of Inquiry. *Science and Children,* 46(2), 26-29.

Bonwell, C.C., Eison, J.A., (1991), Active learning: creating excitement in the classroom. *1991 ASHRE-ERIC Higher Education Report No. 1*. Washington D.C.: The George Washington University, School of Education and Human Development.

Bybee, R. W., & DeBoer, G. (1993). Goals for the Science Curriculum. In *Handbook of Research on Science Teaching and Learning*. Washington, DC: National Science Teachers Association.

DeBoer, G. E. (1991). *A History of Ideas in Science Education: Implications for Practice*. New York: Teachers College Press, Columbia University.

Dewey, J. [1933 (1910)]. *How We Think*. Lexington, MA: D.C. Heath.

Fensham, P. (2008). *Science education policy-making*. Paris: UNESCO.

Herron, M. D. (1971). The nature of scientific inquiry. *School Review* 79, 171-212.

Krajcik, J., Blumenfeld, P., Marx, R., & Soloway, E. (2000). Instructional, curricular, and technological supports for inquiry in science classrooms. In J. Minstrell & E. H. van Zee (Eds.), *Inquiry into inquiry learning and teaching in science* (pp. 283–315). Washington, DC: American Association for the Advancement of Science

Michael Fitzgerald, M., Danaia, L., McKinnon, D. (2019). Barriers Inhibiting Inquiry-Based Science Teaching and Potential Solutions: Perceptions of Positively Inclined Early Adopters. *Research in Science Education*. 49: 543–566 DOI 10.1007/s11165-017-9623-5

National Research Council (2000). Inquiry and the National Science Education Standards: A Guide for Teaching and Learning. Washington, DC: The National Academies Press. https://doi.org/10.17226/9596.

Schwab, J. J. (1962). The teaching of science as enquiry. In J. J. Schwab & P. Brandwein (Eds.), *The teaching of science*. Cambridge, MA: Harvard University Press.

CHAPTER 7: WHAT IS THE GOAL OF A SCIENCE CLASSROOM

Currently, there is consensus within the literature that science, technology, engineering, and mathematics (STEM) education are necessary to facilitate economic development, international competitiveness, and job creation. Certainly, what is needed to meet these goals requires the identification and training of individuals who will enter the professions of science and technology. These professionals will direct the economics of the nation, while improving the personal health of its citizens. Equally important is the need for non-scientists to become scientifically literate to become informed consumers of information that is rich in science and technology, to support a more sustainable vision of growth (Fensham, 2008). Given these two seemingly disparate views, where does this leave science teachers in our quest to prepare students for a future steeped in science and technology? Perhaps a better question to ask is, “How are we currently doing?”

Current Status of Scientific Literacy

Certainly, there is concern given the current level of scientific literacy within this country. For example, the National Science Board (2006) reports that a host of stakeholders (e.g., business, industry, & government agencies) proclaim that to increase this Nation’s opportunities in a global marketplace, efforts to increase educational opportunities for all students must occur. These calls to action resonate in an environment where K-12 education has been challenged with its inadequacies.

Currently, thirty percent of students entering post-secondary institutions require remedial coursework (National Academy of Science, 2007). Moreover, comparisons of scientific literacy against other industrialized nations (National Center for Education Statistics, 2004; Organization for Economic Co-operation and Development, 2007) reveal American students have fallen short of the mark. In fact, within the U.S., recent reports suggest that though much progress has been made in scientific literacy, considerable work remains undone (National Center for Education Statistics, 2004; Organization for Economic Co-operation and Development, 2009). According to the Programme for International Student Assessment, (PISA) which compared 15-year-olds on their math, reading and science skills in 34 of the world’s industrialized countries (OECD, 2018). In the three measures (reading, mathematics, and science), American 15-year-old students placed in the middle half to lower third of the group depending on the specific disciplines tested. According to the 2018 results of PISA for scientific literacy, the United States ranked 18th (behind Poland, Slovenia, and Estonia) and only slightly above the mean. Looking at these scores from a long-range perspective the scores for science in the U.S. have remained flat. From this data, we should not assume everyone else is doing well and we are doing poorly.

In other research (Miller, 2007) performed on adults over the past 20 years has also supplied a slightly different perspective. As of 2005, the highest level of scientific literacy, globally, was found in Sweden (35%), with the U.S. placing second with a scientific literacy rate of 28%. To place second provides little solace given most U.S. citizens remain scientifically illiterate, despite two decades of gains. This contrast in results begs the question, why are adults by comparison more scientifically literate than 15-year-old students?

Visions of Scientific Literacy

The differences between scientific literacy levels of secondary students and adult respondents are credited to the American university system, which requires one year of science for all students, regardless of major (Hobson, 2008). While these increases are encouraging for those adults who matriculate through college coursework, they could hardly be considered a satisfactory level for living in a technological society (Hazen, 2002) and frankly reflect the urgency about scientific literacy felt by the science education community, both nationally and internationally.

Part of the problem may be what we are testing? Administrators of the 2009 PISA announced the test would be designed to go beyond simple recall of scientific knowledge. Instead, the new test design would measure students' ability to identify scientific issues, to explain phenomena scientifically, and to use scientific evidence in real life situations (OECD, 2007). Sadler and Zeidler (2009) criticized test items used in PISA as typical decontextualized (Vision I type) questions within an unnecessary background story. As well, Miller (2007) used a set of core knowledge and process questions. This reveals a crucial point about scientific literacy and how it has been tested. What does it mean to be scientifically literate remains a definitional challenge?

Defining Scientific Literacy

"Scientific literacy" is a term often used in science education, but one that lacks a clear definition (Huling, 2014). Despite being heralded as a world-wide educational outcome, scientific literacy lacks definitional consensus (McEneaney, 2003). Bybee, Fensham, and Laurie (2009) note how deceptively simple scientific literacy may sound, masking its true complexity. As stated by Abd-El-Khalik and Akerson (2004), the development of coherent themes for science education reform, such as scientific literacy based upon previous reform frameworks (AAAS, 1989, NRC, 1996), can serve as an important general guide for student achievement; these reform documents nevertheless distort the vision that scientific literacy has a uniform definition.

For example, the authors of the National Science Education Standards Overview (NRC, 1996) in their opening pages explain why it is so critical for students to become scientifically literate:

- We need scientific information to make choices in our daily lives.
- Important issues that involve science and technology require informed public debate.
- The collective decisions of an informed citizenry will determine how we manage vital natural resources such as air, water, and forests.
- There is personal fulfillment in understanding how the natural world works.
- Science contributes to vital workplace skills of decision-making, creative thinking, and problem solving.
- To compete on a global scale in the world market, we need a capable citizenry.

Roberts (2011) contends there are differences that exist between two philosophical camps which view scientific literacy as either the science itself (to include the products and processes of science) or as the way science interacts with society (the relevance of science to society) (Miller, 2007; National Science Board, 2006; Roberts, 2011).

Miller (2007) argues that if a person can read an article that involves holes in the ozone layer of the atmosphere (Ozone Holes) or genetic engineering as easily as the sports or leisure page in the New York Times, then one could consider himself scientifically literate. In other words, a person knows enough to live in a society steeped in science and its related technology, but not enough to understand the jargon used by scientists and engineers in professional journals. These views are contrasted by those who believe that to be scientifically literate one must be exposed to, and understand, the mathematical rigors or grasp the complex and specific vocabulary (Hazen, 2002). Most students entering school will not become mathematicians, scientists, or engineers; nevertheless, they will enter a world that will demand an understanding of, and an ability to use, scientific information.

There are yet others that wish to expand this definition even further by including socioscientific issues (SSI). Within this view, it is suggested (Zeidler & Sadler, 2011) suggest any vision of scientific literacy is incomplete unless it includes moral and ethical considerations included within SSI. It is recommended (Zeidler & Sadler, 2011) that to move toward a more progressive view of scientific literacy, students will need to practice within a range of social, and ethical dimensions to make informed decisions (e.g., social justice, tolerance for dissenting voice, mutual respect for cultural differences, and making evidenced-driven decisions).

Increasing Student Literacy

The author's view is that despite the historical and ongoing definitional challenges of scientific literacy, what is needed to achieve either vision (Vision I or II) in terms of pedagogical practices enjoys a more or less universal vision. At present, the favored theoretical framework for science teaching within the science education community is rooted in constructivism (Abd-El-Khlaik & Akerson, 2009) as it mirrors the current consensus of what is known about the acquisition of human knowledge (Yang, Chang, & Hsu,2008). Within a constructivist classroom, the practice of teaching should include hands-on and minds-on interactions that require critical and creative thought processes to solve problems (Huling, 2014). Instruction should not be founded upon memorization from textbooks or acquisition of a set of facts and vocabulary that is later tested using multiple choice assessments (NRC, 1996). Unfortunately, many science classes are taught as reading classes (Britner, 2008), rather than using methods that support positive attitudes about science learning, such as those recognized as student-centered and hands-on (Anderson, 2007) including issues-oriented instruction (McComas, 1997). Most definite is the need to increase scientific literacy amongst the nation's students, but what hinders these attempts may be the teachers themselves. Teachers may not be prepared, either by District professional development or by schools of education, with the knowledge and skills to affect the change required by reform movements to increase the level of student's scientific literacy in ways that reflect a more progressive vision. Within both Vision I and

Vision II for scientific literacy, common ground exists, and it is what is included in the reform documents that govern the direction of science education in the U.S. Scientific literacy is defined in the National Science Education Standards as the ability for students to make informed decisions dealing with science and scientific issues with a lesser emphasis on science as a collection of facts (NRC, 1996).

Conclusions

With the newest set of nationally recognized standards, Zeidler argues (2014) science education may now be swinging not toward, but away from a progressive vision of scientific literacy. What will this mean for our science classrooms? How would this effect our instructional practice? In what ways will it affect test scores if teachers are not in lock step with the practices of assessments? What will society choose as its norm for science education moving forward? Will it mean that every child should be able to describe, explain, and predict natural phenomena (i.e., know how to do science)? Will society choose a broader and arguably more inclusive outcome where students are able to read with understanding articles about science in the popular press and to engage in social conversation about the validity of the conclusions (i.e., know how to utilize scientific knowledge to function in a democratic society)? Whatever the outcome for a direction towards the achievement of scientific literacy, it should include the hands-on minds-on approach, rooted in constructivism (Abd-El-Khlaik & Akerson, 2009), and supported by what is known about knowledge acquisition. (Yang, Chang, & Hsu, 2008).

References:

Abd-El-Khalik, F., & Akerson, V. (2004). Learning as conceptual change: Factors mediating the development of preservice elementary teachers' views of nature of science. Science Education, 88, 785-810.

American Association for the Advancement of Science (AAAS). (1989). Science for all Americans: A project 2061 report on literacy goals in science, mathematics, and technology. Washington, DC: American Association for the Advancement of Science.

Anderson, Ronald D. (2007). Inquiry as an organising theme for science curricula. Abell, Sandra.K. & Lederman, Norman G. (Eds.), Handbook of Research on Science Education (p. 807-830). London. Lawrence Erlbaum Associates, Inc.

Britner, S. L. (2008). Motivation in high school science students: A comparison of gender differences in life, physical, and earth science classes. Journal of Research in Science Teaching, 45, 955-970.

Bybee, R., Fensham, P., & Laurie, R. (2009). Scientific literacy and contexts in PISA 2006. Journal of Research in Science Teaching, 46(8), 862-864.

Fensham, P. (2008). Science education policy-making. Paris: UNESCO.

Hazen, R. (2002). Why Should You Be Scientifically Literate? ActionBioscience.org. Retrieved August 7, 2011 , from http://www.actionbioscience.org/newfrontiers/hazen.html

Hobson, A. (2008). The surprising effectiveness of college scientific literacy courses. The Physics Teacher, 46(7), 404-406.

Huling, M. (2014). The Effects of Teachers' Epistemological Beliefs on Practice. An unpublished dissertation. University of South Florida.

McComas, W. F. (1997, spring). The nature of the laboratory experience: a guide for describing, classifying, and enhancing hands-on activities. CSTA Journal, 6-9.

McEneaney, E. H. (2003). The worldwide cachet of scientific literacy. Comparative Education Review, 47(2), 217–237.

Miller, J. (2007). The impact of college science courses for non-science majors on adult science literacy. A paper presented to a symposium titled "The Critical Role of College Science Courses for Non-Majors" at the annual meeting of the AAAS. San Francisco.

National Academy of Science. (2007). Rising Above the Gathering Storm: Energizing and Employing America for a Brighter Economic Future. Washington, D.C: National Academy Press.

National Center for Education Statistics. (2004). Highlights from the trends in international mathematics and science study (TIMSS) 2003. Washington, DC: U.S. Department of Education.

National Research Council. (1996). National science education standards. Washington, DC: National Academy Press.

National Science Board. (2006). Science and Engineering Indicators 2006, Vol. 1, NSB 06-01, Vol. 2, NSB 06-01A. Arlington, VA: National Science Foundation.

Organization for Economic Co-operation and Development. (2003), Definition and selection of competencies: Theoretical and conceptual foundations (DeSeCo), Summary of the final report "Key Competencies for a Successful Life and a Well-Functioning Society", OECD, Paris.

Organization for Economic Co-operation and Development. (2007). PISA 2006: Science competencies for tomorrow's world. Vol. 1. Retrieved from http://www.oecd.org/pisa/pisaproducts/pisa2006/39703267.pdf

Organization for Economic Co-operation and Development (OECD). (2009). What Students Know and Can Do: Student Performance in Reading, Mathematics and Science. Retrieved from PISA 2009 key findings: http://www.oecd.org/pisa/46643496.pdf

Roberts, D. (2011). Competing Visions of Scientific literacy. In C. Linder, L. Ostman, D. Roberts, P. Wickman, G. Erickson, & A. MacKinnon, (Eds.), Exploring the Landscape of Scientific literacy (pp. 11-27). NewYork: Routledge.

Yang, F., Chang, C. Y., & Hsu, Y. S. (2008). Teacher views about constructivist instruction and personal epistemology: a national study in Taiwan. Educational Studies, 34(5), 527 - 542.

Zeidler, D., & Sadler, T. (2011). An inclusive view of scientific literacy: Core issues and future directions of socioscientific reasoning. In C. Linder, L. Ostman, D. A. Roberts, P. Wickman, G. Erickson, & A. MacKinnon, (Eds.), Exploring the landscape of scientific literacy (pp. 176-192). New York: Routledge.

CHAPTER 8: SCIENCE AND THE ELL

by
Tony De Souza, MBA, Ed.D. & Milt Huling, Ph.D.

Often, many K-12 classroom teachers perceive second language acquisition as problematic to their ELL students' academic learning in both the United States and Canada (Huang, Cunningham, & Finn, 2010). To better understand the challenges an ELL encounters, think about how a native English speaker in in a classroom where a different language is spoken. How would we succeed in such an environment, as well as demonstrate our knowledge given the language and cultural barriers? To make matters worse, assume you know little about the content being taught. This is exactly the situation ELL students are placed into every day. Second language acquisition studies show that ELL students experience considerable struggles in their academics due to their limited English proficiency (Barr, Eslami & Joshi, 2012; Jacobson, Hund & Soto-Mas, 2016; Lakin & Young, 2013; Spilt et al. (2012). As student achievement ranks high on the accountability list in public education (Spilt et al., 2012; Weingarten, 2014), local school districts are encouraged to develop academic values in each State that would promote reforms to help increase student academic performance in schools (Master, Loeb & Wyckoff, 2017; Plecki, Elfers, & Nakamura, 2012). Currently in the U.S., there are over 5 million ELL students in public schools, with the majority being Spanish speaking [77.5%] (NCES, 2020). While English Language Learners may be defined differently by individual State statutes, ELLs can more broadly be defined as students with a different language, academic, and social-emotional needs. A misconception of many is that all ELLs are from other countries, but this may not necessarily be the case. An ELL may not have been born in the United States, but it can also be students whose native language is a language other than English (NCES, 2005). Some of these students will be in your classrooms, so how will you make them feel valued, and help them learn both, a language and content, at the same time?

Language Acquisition

It is an interesting paradox that the more we find out about how language development differs from individual to individual and situation to situation, the more we discover about how it is similar for all. The specific differences shed light on and help us identify the deep general and unifying principles that operate across those specific differences of individual learners and situations. In as much, it can take as many as 5-7 years for an ELL to become proficient in English to a point where their language skills are on par with their peers. This is primarily because virtually, all children effortlessly and naturally learn their native tongue, and many learn at least one additional language, as well. (Flack & Horst, 2018; Marshall & Hobsbaum, 2015). Furthermore, Louwerse, & Ventura (2005) argued that the human mind does not contain a module for language acquisition, instead young children absorb the meaning of words through a set of cognitive abilities that includes the ability to infer intentions.

Obviously, teachers of science cannot wait for the development of language before instruction in science begins and reject the belief that students need to be proficient in literacy and numeracy before science can be learned (Lee & Luykx, 2005). There is also evidence to support the notion that second language acquisition is improved via a context/content-dependent approach (TESOL 2006). Though language development continues throughout life, it is most dramatic in the early years before the child comes to school. Much of a teacher's decisions about how instruction will be scaffolded depends on which level a student is at. For example, a Level 1 student on the TESOL scale should be expected to label a simple diagram of a plant (e.g., stem, leaves, roots, flowers). In contrast, a Level 5 student should be expected to explain the relationship between the parts in terms of reproduction and food production (TESOL 2006).

With the knowledge of a students' level of English language proficiency, teachers can make decisions as to when and how to modify instruction, make accommodations, and adapt assessments accordingly. While adjusting instruction and assessment, it is important to remember that only the language is being modified, to make it more comprehensible and attainable to the student. In essence, no one is more concerned than the science teacher with the "what is there?" in the child's learning environment and with supporting the use of what the child makes of it. This is simply due to the business of being a teacher (Falk, Frisoli & Varni, 2021; Fan, 2022). However, content expectations remain the same for ELLs as their English-speaking peers, regardless of the student's level of language proficiency (Castenada & Bautista, 2011).

Figure 1. Proficiency Levels. (Adapted from TESOL 2006)

Level	Stage	Description
Level 1	Starting	Limited or no understanding of English and able to respond nonverbally
Level 2	Emerging	Able to understand phrases and short sentences and use memorized phrases and groups of words.
Level 3	Developing	Able to understand more complex speech but requires repetition and uses simple sentences.
Level 4	Expanding	Able to communicate day-to-day needs and read independently but has challenges with content comprehension.
Level 5	Bridging	Able to express personal or academic topics fluently. Grammatical errors are minimal.

The successful development of reading comprehension is considered paramount for achieving academic success in literacy skills among elementary grade students (Frey & Fisher, 2012: Kennedy & McLoughlin, 2022). Therefore, besides content, science teachers must also support their ELL students in their proficiency in the English language, such as reading, writing, speaking, and listening. For this to occur, emergent literacy skills require development at an early age because it places children on a trajectory for later overall academic success (Arnold et al., 2012) ELL students are expected to demonstrate these proficiencies in these four domains. Therefore, they must also become part of the instruction within the science classroom (TESOL, 2006). Castaneda & Bautista (2011) describe the skills of listening and reading as receptive skills and as such, require the learners to be actively engaged in the learning process. In contrast, the skills of speaking and writing are productive skills that require extensive practice in oral and written communications. For a student to reach a point where there are considered to be truly proficient, proficiency in all four domains (i.e., listening, reading, speaking & writing) must be demonstrated. The question becomes, how can a science teacher integrate these skills into instruction to not only help students better acquire content knowledge, but also help students gain proficiency in the English language?

One of the many strengths of an inquiry approach to learning for an ELL is that it enables the students to learn by doing (Herr, 2008). Inquiry allows students to learn concepts by limiting the barrier of language. At the same time, it enables students to practice language skills collaboratively with their peers in English or even their native languages. This is especially important given the content specific language students need to learn and use (Deussen, et al., 2008). Within the process of inquiry, students are exposed to all the required domains ELL students must practice and eventually demonstrate. Additionally, through the use of inquiry, ELLs do not only learn about content and domain specific vocabulary, but also the practice of science (Amaral, Garrison, & Klentschy, 2002; Fradd & Lee, 1999; Vanosdall et al., 2007; Warren & Rosebery, 2008) which is a critical aspect of scientific literacy.

Writing

It should be no surprise to anyone that to become a better writer, one must write. One such way to do this within a science classroom is using a science journal. While there are many ways to set up such a journal, the important purpose of the journal is that it provides the students with a place to record essential information, either gained from the teacher or their own thoughts. These ideas can be recorded as pictures and drawings, phrases, and important vocabulary terms. A student may also be asked to keep classwork within the journal, which may include labelling diagrams, and writing one sentence definitions, or for the more advanced students, it may include examples of Claims, Evidence, and Reasoning. While the ELL student may initially struggle with writing, the reciprocal nature of writing and speaking cannot be ignored (Karen Worth et. al., 2009). Further support for providing ELLs opportunities to write come from a longitudinal study that followed ELLs during research on a curriculum emphasizing writing and inquiry. After 5 years in the program ELLs were able to outperform their native English-speaking peers (Amaral, Garrison, & Klentschy, 2002). Writing can help students collect their thoughts before they write. Likewise, students that are engaged in discussion before they write can gain valuable information into how they will frame their own writing.

Speaking

Just as writing requires opportunities to practice, so does speaking. ELLs must be provided opportunities to speak, which can be done in their native language with peers whenever possible. These discussions in a native language aid in the development of better understandings of content, just as they would for English speaking students. There are decades of research based on the work of Lev Vygotsky (1962) to support the idea that learning is a product of social interactions within the classroom (Schreiber & Valle, 2013). It then becomes the teacher's role to facilitate such discussions as a natural part of classroom activities (Powell & Kalina, 2009). Fortunately, within a science classroom, small group or dyad discussions becomes commonplace within the hopefully common inquiry activities, without much need for artificial inducement.

As part of deciding on grouping, there are important considerations to make regarding pairings. It is often beneficial to pair a student with a lower level of proficiency with a peer who shares their native language. This pairing can work if the work is done as a dyad or just a part of a large lab group of 3-4 students. This pairing can also ease the flow of conversation about the science content being learned. In contrast, ELLs with a higher level of proficiency should be paired with proficient English speakers to enhance their proficiency growth (Ballantyne, Sanderman, & Levy 2008). These small group settings used in inquiry can provide a more relaxed atmosphere for students to ask questions and seek explanations (Castaneda & Bautista, 2011), which they may otherwise fear to do within a larger group.

Reading

Research on second language acquisition and reading acquisition suggests that students may transfer some language skills from their home language (Bialystok & Craik, 2010; Palacios & Kibler, 2016). This is made possible due to the high frequency (60%) of English words having either Greek or Latin roots (Freeman and Freeman, 2014).

Readability is another consideration to make when choosing text for ELLs. It is perhaps too much to ask a teacher to rewrite a passage to make it accessible to a student's needs. Research suggests using more complex text accompanied by strategic supports is more beneficial for the learner's outcome (Gibbons, 2002; Walqui, 2006; Walqui & Van Lier, 2010; Billings & Walqui, 2017). There are many different strategies to help ELLs with text, such as those listed below:

Figure 2. Reading Strategies for ELLs

Cloze	Activities where students fill in the blanks in a short reading passage.
Selecting short passages	Read to students first then have them read and look for evidence of comprehension.
Jigsaw	Jigsaw is a cooperative learning strategy that enables different groups to interact with each other. As students learn new content from members in a different group, they take the information and share it with their "home" group. Provide ELLs with additional written, visual, or audio content (e.g., a glossary).
Amplification	The teacher inserts additional information into sentences within the text to support the reader.
Text Dependent Questions (TDQs)	TDQs draw ELs' attention to key language and concepts.
Pre-teach	Use visuals, realia, gestures, student-created definitions, examples and non-examples, synonyms and antonyms, to name a few. (Note: Avoid pre-teaching words whose meaning can quickly be accessed by utilizing clues in the surrounding text.
Gloss vocabulary	Gloss selected words unfamiliar to ELs by highlighting them in a glossary

Technology now provides tools to determine a text's difficulty so a selection can be made more pragmatically. Within Microsoft Word, there is the Flesch-Kinkaid Readability tool that can be used to determine the grade level of the text being considered, taking only seconds. There are also online tools such as Lexile.com that can do a similar function to better align the text to a reader's ability. Depending on the school district, whether it is supportive of a dual language approach, or one solely focused on English only, online translation tools and even the ability to read the text to the student are options that can be considered. Reading using technology can also make it possible to highlight text or copy and paste text when appropriate to answer TDQs.

Listening

Listening is a critical skill for all students because it is linked to reading and writing, but particularly for ELLs as they are acquiring both content and a new language. This is especially true for those still in the silent stage and are not yet capable of producing speech in English. This stage must be respected and approached in a non-threatening manner, but that does not mean they are not participating in other instructional activities. For example, hands-on learning exposes the student to an environment where they can learn the content, but also experience hearing ideas from their peers. The groups they are placed in may include speakers of their native language, but not exclusively as they may limit their exposure to hearing English as a second language (Tsang, 2021).

Figure 3. Language Acquisition Tool Kit (Adapted from Herr 2008)

Language-based science games	used to reinforce/review vocabulary
Picture glossary	used to help students associate concepts with words.
Root words	used to help students better understand English. Prefixes and suffixes should also be included in this instruction.
Cognates	words that are similar in two or more languages.
Word wall	Post new vocabulary terms on the wall.
Emphasize visual literacy	the ability to evaluate, apply, or create conceptual visual representations.
Graphic Organizers	are diagrams or maps that show the relationship between new and existing concepts, thereby facilitating integration of new and familiar ideas.
Use charts, graphs, & figures	can communicate concepts with minimal use of spoken or written language. The layout of such visual aids should be clear and uncluttered.

Before children are ready to speak, they should be encouraged to point, identify, act out, and illustrate their knowledge as a way to demonstrate their comprehension. Other ways to help students that are still developing speaking skills due to limited English proficiency may also include choral readings, echo reading, shared reading and writing, and singing. It may also be beneficial to not always place ELLs together in the same group to provide greater exposure to proficient English speakers. When students are able to start language production in English, at least for a portion of the lesson, ELL students should be placed in groups with only native English speakers so that they are motivated to use their new language (Weimer, 2001).

Conclusions

Content area teachers must take initiative and seek knowledge and resources for teaching ELLs in their classrooms. Additionally, acquiring English as a second language for ELLs in K-12 classrooms requires teachers to show that they are valued. In doing so will help these students learn both, a language and content at the same time. For many ELLs, it may take 5-7 years for English language proficiency to transpire, and teachers of science cannot wait for the development of this proficiency to reach maturity before instruction in science is given. Scaffolding lessons is a great way to help teachers make decisions on when to modify their lessons for ELLs and make accommodations and adaptations appropriately. In doing so will make science instruction more comprehensible and attainable for the learner. Furthermore, the successful development of reading comprehension in science education is paramount for an ELL to achieve academic success as this makes the needed connection between content and their literacy skills. Science education is also naturally conducive for ELLs to use an inquiry approach to learning as it enables students to learn by doing. This process fosters concept learning by limiting the language barrier. Reading, writing, speaking, and listening are fundamental skills for all children in early literacy development and is an imperative stage for an English language learner acquiring language proficiency skills in school.

References:

Amaral, O. M., Garrison, L., & Klentschy, M. (2002). Helping English learners increase achievement through inquiry-based science instruction. *Bilingual Research Journal 26*(2): 213–239.

Arnold., D. H., Kupersmidt, J. B., Voegler-Lee, M. E., & Marshall, N. A. (2012). The association between preschool children's social functioning and their emergent academic skills. *Early Childhood Research Quarterly, 27*(3), 376-386.

Ballantyne, K.G., Sanderman, A.R., & Levy, L. (2008). *Educating English language learners: Building teacher capacity.* Washington, DC: National Clearinghouse for English Language Acquisition.

Barr, S., Eslami, Z., & Joshi, R. (2012). Core strategies to support English language learners. Education Forum, 76(1), 105-117.

Bialystok, E., & Craik, F. I. M. (2010). Cognitive and linguistic processing in the bilingual mind. *Current Directions in Psychological Science, 19*, 19-23.

Billings, E. & Walqui, A. (2017). Topic brief 5: Dispelling the myth of "English only": understanding the importance of the first language in second language learning. New York State Education Department. Retrieved from http://www.nysed.gov/bilingualed/topic-brief-5-dispelling-myth-english-only-understanding-importance-first-language

Castaneda, M. & Bautista, N. (2011). Teaching Science to ELLs: Part II. *The Science Teacher*. 78. 40-44.

Deussen, T., Autio, E., Miller, B., Turnbaugh-Lockwood, A., and Stewart, V. (2008). *What Teachers Should Know About Instruction for English Language Learners*. Center for Research, Evaluation, and Assessment. Education Northwest. Portland, OR.

Falk, D., Frisoli, P., & Varni, E. (2021). The importance of teacher well-being for student mental health and resilient education systems. *Forced Migration Review, 66,* 17-21.

Fan, S. -C. (2022). An important-performance analysis (IPA) of teachers' core competencies for implementing maker education in primary and secondary schools. *International Journal of Technology & Design Education, 32*(2), 943-969.

Farah, R., Meri, R., Kadis, D. S., Hutton, J., DeWitt, T., & Horowitz-Kraus, T. (2019). Hyperconnectivity during screen-based stories listening is associated with lower narrative comprehension in preschool children exposed to screens vs dialogic reading: An EEG study. *PLoS ONE, 14*(11), 1-16.

Flack, Z. M., & Horst, J. S. (2018). Two sides to every story: Children learn words better from one storybook page at a time. *Infant & Child Development, 27*(1), 1.

Frey, N., & Fisher, D. (2012). Reading in every classroom, every day. *Principal Leadership, 12*(6). 58-60.

Fradd, S. H., & Lee, O. (1999). Teachers' roles in promoting science inquiry with students from diverse language backgrounds. *Educational Researcher* 28 (6): 4–20, 42.

Freeman, D. E. & Freeman, Y. S. (2014). *Essential linguistics*. Heinemann.

Gibbons, P. (2002). Learning language, learning through language, and learning about language: Developing an integrated curriculum. In *Scaffolding Language, Scaffolding Learning: Teaching Second Language, Learners in the Mainstream Classroom*. pp 118-138. Portsmouth, NH: Heinemann

Herr, N. (2008). *The sourcebook for teaching science, grades 6-12: strategies, activities, and Resources*. Josey Bass, San Francisco, CA.

Huang, J., Cunningham, J., & Finn, A. (2010). Teacher perceptions of ESOL students' greatest challenges in academic English skills: A k-12 perspective. *International Journal of Applied Educational Studies, 8*(1), 68-80.

Jacobson, H. E., Hund, L., & Soto-Mas, F. (2016). Predictors of English health literacy among U.S. hispanic immigrants: The importance of language, bilingualism and sociolinguistic environment. *Literacy & Numeracy Studies, 24*(1), 43-65.

Kennedy, C., & McLoughlin, A. (2022). Developing the emergent literacy skills of English language learners through dialogic reading: A systematic review. *Early Childhood Education Journal,* 1-6.

Kuhl, P. (2011). Early language learning and literacy: Neuroscience implications for education. *Mind Brain and Education, 5*(3), 42-128.

Lakin, J. M., & Young, J. W. (2013). Evaluating growth for ELL students: Implications for accountability policies. *Issues & Practice, 32*(3), 11-26.

Lee, O., and Luykx, A. (2005). Dilemmas in scaling up educational innovations with nonmainstream students in elementary school science. *American Educational Research Journal* 43: 411–438.

Louwerse, M. M., & Ventura, M. (2005). How children learn the meaning of words and how LSA does it (too). *Journal of the Learning Sciences, 14*(2), 301-309.

Marshall, C. R., & Hobsbaum, A. (2015). Sign-supported English: Is it effective at teaching vocabulary to young children with English as an additional language? *International Journal of Language & Communication Disorders, 50*(5), 616-628.

Master, B., Loeb, S., & Wyckoff, J. (2017). More than content: The persistent cross-subject effects of English language arts teachers' instruction. *Educational Evaluation and Policy Analysis, 39*(3), 429-447.

National Center for Education Statistics (2020). State Nonfiscal Survey of Public Elementary and Secondary Education, 2018–19. Washington. D.C. U.S. Department of Education. retrieved December 8, 2021 @ https://nces.ed.gov/programs/digest/d20/tables/dt20_204.27.asp?

National Center for Educational Statistics (2005). *Characteristics of the 100 largest public elementary and secondary school districts* 2001-2002. Washington. D.C. U.S. Department of Education.

Palacios, N., & Kibler, A. (2016). Oral English language proficiency and reading mastery: The role of home language and school support. *Journal of Educational Research, 109*(2). 122-136.

Plecki, M. L., Elfers, A. M., & Nakamura, Y. (2012). Using evidence for teacher education program improvement and accountability: An illustrative case of the role of value-added measures. *Journal of Teacher Education, 63*(5), 318-334. doi:10.1177/0022487112447110

Powell, K., & Kalina, K., (2009). Cognitive and social constructivism: Developing tools for an effective classroom. Education 130(2)

Schreiber, L. M., & Valle, B. E. (2013). Social constructivist teaching strategies in the small group classroom. *Small Group Research*, *44*(4), 395–411. https://doi.org/10.1177/1046496413488422

Spilt, J. L., Hughes, J. N., Wu, J., & Kwok, O. (2012). Dynamics of teacher-student relationships: stability and change across elementary school and the influence on children's academic success. *Child Development*, *83*(4), 1180-1195. doi:10.1111/j.1467-8624.2012.01761.x

Teachers of English to Speakers of Other Languages [TESOL] (2006). TESOL revises preK–12 English language proficiency standards. www.tesol.org/s_TESOL/sec_document.asp?CID=1445&DID=5349#levels

Tsang, A. (2021). The road not taken: Greater emphasis needed on "sounds", "actual listening", and "spoken input." *RELC Journal,* 1.

Vanosdall, R., Klentschy, M., Hedges, L.V., & Weisbaum, K.S. (2007). *A randomized study of the effects of scaffolded guided-inquiry instruction on student achievement in science.* Paper presented at the annual meeting of the American Educational Research Association, Chicago, IL.

Vygotsky, L.S. (1962). Thought and language. Cambridge, MA: *MIT Press* (original work published in 1934).

Walqui, A. (2006). Scaffolding instruction for English language learners: A conceptual framework. *International Journal of Bilingual Education and Bilingualism, 9*(2), 159-180, doi: 10.1080/13670050608668639

Walqui, A., & van Lier, L. (2010). A Pedagogy of Promise. *Scaffolding the academic success of adolescent English language learners: A pedagogy of promise*. San Francisco: WestEd. Retrieved from: http://www.WestEd.org/scaffoldingacademicsuccess

Warren, B., & Rosebery, A. (2008). Using everyday experience to teach science. In *Teaching science to English language learners*, eds. A. Rosebery and B. Warren, 39–50. Arlington, VA: NSTA Press.

Weingarten, R. (2014). International education comparisons: How American education reform is the new status quo. *New England Journal of Public Policy*, *26*(1), 1-10.

WIDA (2012). *2012 Amplifications of English Language Development Standards. Kindergarten -Grade 12*. Madison, WI: University of Wisconsin.

Weiner, (2001). *Preparing for Success: Meeting the Language and Learning Needs of Young Children from Poverty Homes*. ECL Publications. Youngtown, AZ.

Worth, K., Winokuer, J., Crisman, S., Heller-Winokur, M., & Davis, M., (2009). *The Essentials of Science and Literacy: A Guide for Teachers.* Heinemann, London.

CHAPTER 9: SCIENCE AND ESE

The passage of the Individuals with Disabilities Act in 1997, quickly followed by the passage of No Child Left Behind Act (2001), served to establish the mandate to provide greater inclusion for students with special needs in classrooms. The objective of these mandates is to provide the least restrictive environment for these students. Based on the data from the National Center for Education Statistics (2017), there are over six million students with disabilities in the United States. For teachers, it is essential to meet the instructional needs for each diverse learner. It is important for today's educators to understand the barriers associated with each type of learning challenge. It is, also, important for science teachers to consider these unique challenges when determining the best approach to providing science instruction for each student.

Understanding Instructional Disabilities

Traditionally, a student labeled as having a disability can include those students with physical, cognitive, or even social-emotional impairments that influences activities in their daily lives. Physical impairments can include deficits in one's visual, auditory, fine, and gross motor skills. Cognitive impairments can include, but are not limited to, dyslexia, dyscalculia, dysgraphia, and developmental aphasia.

Table 1. Cognitive Impairment Definitions

Dyslexia	a learning disorder that involves difficulty reading due to problems identifying speech sounds and learning how they relate to letters and words (i.e., decoding).
Dyscalculia	a learning difficulty that affects an individual's ability to do basic arithmetic such as addition, subtraction, multiplication, and division. Estimation skills can also be affected.
Dysgraphia	a condition that affects the ability to write letters by hand.
Aphasia	a disorder that affects how you communicate. It can impact your speech & writing, as well as the understanding of both spoken and written language.

Children can also suffer from a lack of social and emotional skills (Comer, 1988). Children with social-emotional learning disabilities (SELD) are defined as those students who have chronic difficulty relating to others. Children with this disability often misinterpret the emotional responses of others making it difficult to negotiate and compromise in social settings. They may struggle to manage frustration, struggle to pay attention in class, lack self-confidence and struggle to establish positive and rewarding relationships with their peers. Given the plethora of potential disabilities, is it any wonder teachers may feel inadequately prepared.

Academic Achievement in Science

It is interesting to note that the U.S. efforts for full inclusion far exceed the inclusion policies of other industrialized nations. While a seemingly daunting task to meet the instructional needs of the diverse learners, the good news may be that science provides a great discipline in which to meet these needs. Science, and its best practices, such as hands-on experiential learning, collaboration with peers, incorporating alternate ways of demonstrating ideas and knowledge are the hallmarks of best practices for science instruction as they are engaged in inquiry (Taylor et al., 2012). Unfortunately, even with the benefits that reside within the best practices for science instruction, there are persistent problems that impact student performance (Steele, 2004).

Science Teacher Preparedness

With the 2001 passage of the No Child Left Behind (NCLB) Act, many institutions of higher learning place an emphasis on the student teachers' acquisition of math and reading instructional practices and not the acquisition of science instruction. Regretfully, it is seldom when the science methods course(s) address the teaching of science to students with disabilities (Norman, Caseau, & Stefanich, 1998; Irving, Nti, & Johnson, 2007). While teachers receive limited preparation in the teaching of science compared to math and reading, they describe their feelings of inadequacy to teach students with special needs within their general education classroom. (Soodak, Podell, & Lehman, 1998).

One approach that may help a teacher navigate the needs of their students is to consider students labeled with a disability as merely being neurologically diverse needing only a different type of instruction versus findings ways to "fix them." In the late 1990s, Judy Singer, a sociologist, who is on the autism spectrum herself, came up with a word *"neurodiversity"* to describe conditions like ADHD, Autism, and Dyslexia. Her goal was to shift the dialogue away from terms such as deficits, disorders, and impairments. Students with no neurological conditions are neurotypical. Students with neurological conditions are referred to neurodiverse and are merely a result of normal variations of the human genome (Singer, 2017). While critics of the neurodiversity argue the term is skewed toward higher functioning individuals, especially in terms of autism, it is those higher functioning individuals who would be placed in traditional inclusive science classrooms. As these diverse learners can have strengths (e.g., the ability to hyper focus, creativity, innovation, unique perspectives, etc.) as well as weaknesses, what is the best approach to instruction to accommodate their needs (Disabled World, 2022)?

Pedagogical Frameworks

One thing is certain, utilizing the traditional textbook is not a good instructional approach for students with disabilities (Cawley & Parmar, 2001). Methods based in print, in general, may not provide a strong instructional option if the teachers do not address the accessibility needs of the student (Pisha & Stahl, 2005). Teachers must find methods of delivery to make science accessible for all students, including those students with disabilities (Kahn, Pigman, & Ottley, 2017). One recommended approach is through the implementation of the pedagogical framework of Universal Design for Learning [UDL] (Meyer, Rose, & Gordon, 2014). By utilizing UDL, teachers can develop learning environments that provide the necessary flexibility needed so that all students can become participants in their learning. It is suggested (Kahn, et al., 2017) that UDL enables the teacher to develop lessons that engage students, provide a feasible means of demonstrating knowledge in a way that reduces barriers in a proactive manner versus adding accommodations retroactively, thereby maximizing access and participation. The pedagogical framework of UDL is now seen as a vital tool in planning and implementing instruction for students with disabilities and is now endorsed as a research-based instructional approach (ESSA, 2015, NETP, 2016).

The UDL Science Classroom

Universal Design for Learning (UDL) is a valuable tool in a teacher's arsenal for planning lessons. UDL is a framework that can improve academic success by better aligning instruction to what is known about how students learn. This is accomplished by finding means of stimulating student interest, utilizing different modes of instruction, and allowing students to express their knowledge in formats that meet their strengths and interest (Rose & Meyer, 2002).

Using the UDL principles, science teachers are able to design lessons that can more effectively meet learning needs of a diverse classroom. This is accomplished by designing lessons where students have flexibility in both how they access information as well as how they demonstrate their knowledge. The UDL framework is built around three guiding principles: Representation, Action/Expression, and Engagement.

In terms of representation, a science teacher in the 20th century has multiple options for how students access information. One common method is the textbook, but students can also access information through various types of written text, such as realistic fiction. Other means of accessing these same types of written text may be through text to speech options or video clips. Perhaps the method most familiar to science teachers is through a hands-on learning approach or even a digital version of hands-on labs using simulations.

How students demonstrate their knowledge can also be differentiated in a science classroom. Perhaps the most common way students express what they know is through paper and pencil assessments at the end of a lesson or unit. Why not allow students to create a presentation using PowerPoint (PPT), or another digital tool? Students can also create written responses by writing a story or creating a comic strip.

In terms of engagement, the inquiry methodology makes learning more engaging than merely reading a textbook and answering the questions at the end of the chapter. As well, providing relevance by adding a phenomenological or sociological component can make the inquiry-based lesson more relevant and engaging to the student. Other strategies may include gamification strategies impose on certain components of the lessons, which may include, games of memory to solidify vocabulary and content, or jeopardy-style games.

Recent research (Kahn, et al, 2017) investigated how teachers view lesson creation that include students with disabilities. The study noted how teacher candidates created lesson plans that could be placed into two categories, that of 'doing for' or 'doing with' students with disabilities. The researchers (Kahn, et al. 2017) stated how a 'doing for' mindset may be ultimately damaging to a student with a disability as it provides "fewer opportunities to gain autonomy and develop the skills needed to progress in science (p. 61)." Examples of 'doing for' might include have premade items versus having students cut them out, or having another student complete a task while the student with a disability only watches or has the activity explained to them. If the goal is for students to learn from one another in a collaborative environment, then they need to be able to exercise their ability to participate and share their experiences in an equitable manner without being singled out. By providing flexibility, UDL allows students to engage in learning in ways that best meets their needs and interest.

What Now?

While students with disabilities struggle to participate in classroom activities and in completing assignments, what are some specific things teachers can do? How can the classroom environment and the lessons taught within it be modified accordingly and accommodations be put in place as needed? In the science classroom, just like any other setting, students with disabilities must be provided on an individualized basis with any necessary accommodations and modification required to be an active participant in the learning experience. Appropriate accommodations depend on the type of disability (I.e., physical, intellectual, learning, or sensory). It should be emphasized; the goal is to have the experience individualized as disabilities vary greatly.

The University of Washington (2010) has developed a list of questions that can help determine the types of modification and accommodations that may be required:

1. What does this exercise or assignment require?
2. What physical, intellectual, and sensory skills are needed?
3. What components of the exercise or assignment require accommodations?
4. What accommodation options exist?

First, it is important to distinguish between accommodation, modification, and differentiation.

- Accommodations are adaptations that provided an access point to students who might otherwise have barriers. Adaptations can be necessary for ESE and traditional students. It is important to note that these adaptations or accommodations do not alter the curriculum (Jung, 2018). An example of a common accommodation in a science classroom might be providing extended time to complete tasks.
- Modification requires a fundamental change in the curriculum, such as outcome expectations (Zollman, 2016). Ways to modify instruction may include changes to the readability of text as either leveled or adapted. Other methods of modification may include a limit of the content knowledge required to learn or presenting content that is different than the standard curriculum.
- Differentiation is planned curriculum that takes into consideration the individual needs or interests of the child by providing them both a voice and a choice. As Tomlinson (2018) states, "Differentiation means tailoring instruction to meet individual needs."

Conclusions

Accommodation, modification, and differentiation are adaptations that help cater to the individual needs of a learner. Where accommodation is about how instruction is delivered and modification is about what a child will learn, differentiation focus on how a child will demonstrate learning. By using all three in conjunction, the learning environment can make the learning, as well as the demonstration of the learning, more accessible. At the same time, it makes it possible to recognize the unique strengths and weaknesses of the individual students in your classroom.

Perhaps the most important thing to remember when a teacher of science is planning for or teaching students with disabilities, modification, and accommodations should be made so that the least restrictive environment is obtained. This has profound implications for inquiry-based science where the goal is for students to experience the learning as much as possible, not have it demonstrated to them unless absolutely necessary. As Kahn (2017) argues, it is always best to find the middle ground between inclusion and exclusion. In other words, do not rush to "do for" a student when possible, allowing them to be a participant in the science classroom and not exclude them to an observer status.

References:

Cawley, J., Foley, T., & Miller, J. (2003). Science and students with mild disabilities: Principles of universal design. *Intervention in School and Clinic,* 38(3), 160–171.

Cole, C., & McLesky, J. (1997). Secondary inclusion programs for students with mild disabilities. *Focus on Exceptional Children,* 29(6), 1–15.

Disabled World. (2022, May 29). What Is: Neurodiversity, Neurodivergent, Neurotypical. *Disabled World*. Retrieved July 13, 2022 from www.disabled-world.com/disability/awareness/neurodiversity/

Every Student Succeeds Act, 20 U.S.C. § 6301 (2015). https://www.congress.gov/bill/114th-congress/senate-bill/1177

Individuals with Disabilities Education Act Amendments, Public Law 105-17. (June 4, 1997).

Individuals with Disabilities Education Act, 20 U.S.C. § 1400 (2004).

Irving, M., Nti, M., & Johnson, W. (2007). Meeting the needs of the special learner in science. International Journal of Special Education, 22(3), 109–118. Retrieved from http://files.eric.ed.gov/fulltext/EJ814520.pdf

Jung, L. A. (2018). Is It an Accommodation or a Modification? *ASCD Student Growth Center*. N.p., 07 June 2017. Web. 02 Feb. 2018.

Kahn, S., Pigman, R., & Ottley, J. (2017). A Tale of Two Courses: Exploring Teacher Candidates' Translation of Science and Special Education Methods Instruction Into Inclusive Science Practices.

Meyer, A., Rose, D., & Gordon, D. (2014). Universal design for learning: Theory and practice. Wakefield, MA: CAST Publications.

National Center for Education Statistics. (2017). Children and Youth with Disabilities. Washington, DC: Institute of Education Sciences, U.S. Department of Education. Retrieved from https://nces.ed.gov/programs/coe/indicator_cgg.asp

National Education Technology Plan. (2016). Future ready learning: Reimagining the role of technology in education. U.S. Department of Education: Office of Educational Technology Retrieved from https://tech.ed.gov/files/2015/12/NETP16.pdf

No Child Left Behind Act of 2001, H.R.1 - 107th Congress (2001-2002). Retrieved 11/13/2021 @ https://www.congress.gov/bill/107th-congress/house-bill/1

Pisha, B., & Stahl, S. (2005). The promise of new learning environments for students with disabilities. *Intervention in School and Clinic*, 41(1), 67–75.

Qualifications and Curriculum Authority. (2001). Science. *Planning, teaching and assessing the curriculum for pupils with learning difficulties*. London: OCA.

Rose, David H; Meyer, Anne (2002). *Teaching every student in the digital age: universal design for learning*. Alexandria, VA: Association for Supervision and Curriculum Development. ISBN 0-87120-599-8. OCLC 49994086.

Singer, J. (2017). NeuroDiversity: The Birth of an Idea. [publisher not identified]. Lexington, Kentucky:

Soodak, L., Podell, D., & Lehman, L. (1998). Teacher, student, and school attributes as predictors of teachers' responses to inclusion. *The Journal of Special Education*, 31(4), 480–497.

Taylor, J. C., Therrien, W. J., Kaldenberg, E., Watt, S., Chanlen, N., & Hand, B. (2012). Using an inquiry-based teaching approach to improve science outcomes for students with disabilities: snapshot and longitudinal data. Journal of Science Education for Students with Disabilities, 15(1), 27-39. doi:10.14448/jsesd.04.0003

Tomlinson, C. A. (2018). What Is Differentiated Instruction, *Reading Rockets*. N.p., 31 Dec. 2015. Web. 02 Feb. 2018.

University of Washington. (2010). Disabilities, Opportunities, Internetworking & Technology. Retrieved June 24, 2010, from www.washington.edu/doit/

Zollman, E. M. (2018). Accommodations vs. Modifications: What's The Difference?, *Handy Handout* N.p., n.d. Web. 02 Feb. 2018.

CHAPTER 10: PLANNING FOR ACADEMIC SUCCESS

In this age of accountability, high stakes tests often determine a student's future course track, promotion, or even the type of diploma they receive upon graduation (e.g., Honors or Traditional). These factors make such assessments critical for determining students' academic futures. Because of these consequences, teachers are left to figure out how best to meet their students' needs and find a balance between preparing them for assessments, but also helping develop the deep understandings of content that have become a mainstay of science reform movements (NRC, 1996; NRC, 2012). The question we must all ask ourselves is, are teachers of science left with a dichotomous choice of simply covering content and test-prep or to deliver the type of instruction we know as "good" teaching?

An all-too-common refrain from teachers is, "We now have to teach to the test," but what does this really mean in practice? In many cases it means a switch away from ways of teaching that are aligned to what the science education community knows about how students learn (i.e., constructivism). In other words, a transformation in instructional approaches, such as inquiry, toward one that is based on the use of test preparation materials aimed solely at increasing test scores and not improving students' understandings of concepts or the mastery of skills (Shepard 1990). "Covering the material" can often generate images of lecture, again promoting a shift away from best practices associated with student learning (McGlynn, 2020). This begs the question; how can teachers effectively teach the mandated state standards and avoid the pitfalls associated with "teaching to the test" or "covering content?"

The Dreaded Lesson Plans

Perhaps one of the most daunting and time-consuming tasks teachers have as part of their duties is preparing lesson plans. Most schools require teachers to turn in lesson plans to provide evidence that state standards have been covered. Beyond lesson plans as a compliance issue, they are also an important guide for instruction. Lessons can be defined differently by teachers with views now aligned with creating a student-centered environment focused on learning versus "covering standards" or "teaching to the test." To a teacher focused on covering material or standards, a lesson plan may be little more than a list of content to be covered, with some activities included for good measure. To a master teacher, lesson plans are more thought of as the detailed plan designed to provide a learning pathway towards the targeted learning goal, whether that be an understanding of a concept or mastery of a skill. Good lesson plans typically contain a goal for learning, methods of instruction to reach the goal, and a way of knowing if the goal has been met. If this description sounds overly simplistic, it is. Lesson plans can take a teacher many hours to create and require knowledge of both standards, content, and knowledge of pedagogical skills.

Planning Instruction

To create an effective lesson, it is essential to identify what is to be learned, a skill or a concept, as this may determine the approach of the lesson. The next step is to decide on the goal of the lesson, what do we want the student to be able to do because of instruction, this requires looking closely at the standard. Does the standard require simple recall, ability to compare and contrast, evaluate, perform a task, etc.? The type of outcome is vital in determining the lesson target. By starting with the planned outcome, activities, instructional strategies, and assessments (both formative and summative) are then constructed with the end in mind (Hinchliffe, 2016).

McTighe and Wiggins (2005) have developed a framework, called Understanding by Design (UbD) that encourages a backward design process to ensure outcomes are planned for and not just artifacts of the educational process. Using the backward design method, the teacher starts with outcomes based on state mandated standards. Teachers then plan lessons by choosing activities and other appropriately aligned materials to help students construct an understanding of the topic at hand. By using this strategy, teachers can better attain success for their students.

An alternate and more traditional view of lesson planning uses a forward-looking methodology where a list of content that will be taught is created and/or selected. This, more traditional manner, favors a more teacher-centered approach focused on content and not the learning process, thereby placing all responsibility of learning on the student. This choice makes little sense if a teacher is to be thought of as a facilitator of learning and not a disseminator of information that will be on the test.

The criteria to plan lessons using UbD requires teachers to consider the following 3 stages in their planning (McTighe & Wiggins, 2005):

- **Identify Desired Results** (i.e., typically tied to State standards, not test specifications)
- **Determine Acceptable Evidence of Learning** (i.e., what will a student produce or demonstrate)
- **Plan Learning Experiences and Instruction** (i.e., write the lesson to include appropriate pedagogy)

Incorporating UbD into your lesson planning process leads toward a more intentional approach. Furthermore, using UbD provides a teacher with a better idea of student expectations at the culmination of the lesson. UbD also minimizes extraneous activities, that while fun and engaging, may not fit into the goal of the lesson. By thinking first about what you want students to know, the better outcome you will have in providing the types of instruction that meets the needs of the student to be academically successful.

Planning to Meet All Student's Needs

As mentioned in a previous chapter, Universal Design for Learning (UDL) is a highly effective tool that is vital to lesson planning. UDL can increase academic success by allowing students opportunities to choose tasks that are in alignment to their interests and strengths (Rose & Meyer, 2002). UDL should not be confused with a singular or universal way to teach children. Quite the opposite, UDL helps to individualize learning to accommodate the diverse range of student needs.

For planning science lessons, it is important to provide various ways for students to access information as well as how they might demonstrate their learning. To prepare lesson plans that incorporate UDL, consider the following:

- What are your students' strengths and weaknesses?
- What are ways to share information with students?
- What are options for students to demonstrate their knowledge?
- How can software help support learning (e.g., text to speech)?
- Are there Low and No Tech options?

By providing flexibility, UDL allows students to engage in learning in ways that best meets their needs and interest. Furthermore, it allows ways to adapt the learning of content to the learner as opposed to expecting the learner to adapt to the instruction of content.

Conclusions

The goal of science educators is to help their students develop a deeper understanding of content, but how is this accomplished in a system seemingly ruled by high stakes test? To meet this goal requires more than covering content or teaching to the test. Teachers must plan instruction in a way that not just covers content, but also reaches the depth of understanding necessary to meet the intentions of the standard.

By using UbD and UDL, teachers now have the tools to plan instruction to target student outcome. UbD helps teachers target student outcomes, so they are more than a hoped-for artifact of instruction. For this reason, backward design is considered a superior method as compared to the more traditional methods of lesson design. By utilizing the UDL framework, teachers can now create instructional pathways that better accommodate the learning needs of ALL students, while not altering the curriculum in terms of depth, breadth, or difficulty. By combining the practices of UbD with the framework of UDL, teachers now have the tools to teach in a manner that goes far beyond teaching to the test, while still providing a means for students to be academically successful.

References:

Hinchliffe, L.J. (2016). Instructional Design for Literacy: Using the "Understanding by Design" Model to Achieve Learner Success. Available online at: https://iflasatellitetampere2012.files.wordpress.com/2012/08/session6b_hinchliffe.pdf 7.

Llewellyn, D. (2005). *Teaching High School Science Through Inquiry*, Thousand Oaks, CA: Corwin Press.

McGlynn, T. (2020). *The Chicago Guide to College Science Teaching*, The University of Chicago Press. London.

National Research Council. (1996). National science education standards. Washington, DC: National Academy Press.

National Research Council. (2012). A Framework for K-12 Science Education: Practices, Crosscutting Concepts, and Core Ideas. Washington, DC: The National Academy Press.

Rose, D. H., & Meyer, A (2002). *Teaching every student in the digital age: universal design for learning*. Alexandria, VA: Association for Supervision and Curriculum Development. ISBN 0-87120-599-8. OCLC 49994086.

Shepard, L.A. (2000). The role of assessment in a learning culture. Presidential Address presented at the annual meeting of the American Educational Research Association, New Orleans, April 26.

Wiggins, G. & McTighe, J. (2005). *Understanding by Design. Expanded 2nd Edition*. (Upper Saddle River, NJ/Alexandria, VA: Pearson Education/Association for Supervision & Curriculum Development.

CHAPTER 11: LEARNING MODELS

Problem

Instructional models have had a long history in education. Over the years, researchers have attempted to determine how best to align instruction based on what is known about how children learn. In Florida, most districts have chosen to use the Gradual Release Model (GRM) for ELA and the 5E Instructional Model for math and science, both based in constructivism. Constructivism as a method of teaching has become a predominant theoretical rationale for developing applications for instruction (Moon, 1999), in other words, "best practices." The problem the author has noticed with his background as a teacher, K-12 district office administrator, and college professor, is there remains much confusion over when, where, and how, to correctly apply these tools of the trade in a meaningful and effective manner.

Gradual Release Defined

The gradual release model was first introduced in 1983 by Pearson & Gallagher. The process of instruction is based on the notion that instruction should transition from explicit modeling and instruction, to guided practice, and then to activities that students complete independently. The model uses Vygotsky's ideas of instruction where the teacher acts like a tour guide or mentor to facilitate higher levels of thinking within the Zone of Proximal Development (1978). It is this "More Knowledgeable Other (MKO)" that facilitates and scaffolds instruction for the learner, with the goal for the student to become an independent learner, no longer needing the teacher.

Lesson "Hook"

While technically not a part of the GRM, many teachers use a hook to engage students at the opening of a lesson. The 'Hook' can help to grab the students' attention, as well as to frame the thinking and to promote focus on the upcoming lesson. Essentially, lesson hooks help students make connections between existing knowledge and the learning objective.

I Do

Within the "I DO" portion of the GRM, the teacher will follow a precise pattern of modelling (Fisher & Frey, 2008a). Fisher and Frey (2008a) make the claim that for students to be successful, students must gain deeper understandings for when to apply, watch for, and recognize ways to analyze their own success. Within this "I Do" portion of the lesson, students listen while the teacher/facilitator models their own thinking. For example, students may hear the teacher say, "I think...", or "I wonder...", or "I predict. The key thing to keep in mind is student-centered, not teacher centered. The teacher should be demonstrating how, by making obvious their own thinking process, not simply telling students what to do.

We Do

This phase of the GRM generally has two components, guided and collaborative.

- Guided Instruction- The teacher guides and releases more responsibility to the students as they work towards a more accurate utilization of the newly obtained skill using questions, prompts, and cues. In this phase the student no longer needs the teacher as a model, rather they need support or instructional scaffolds as they attempt their own application. It is also within this portion of the lesson where differentiation occurs through the utilization of small groups.
- Collaborative/Productive Instruction - This portion of the GRM requires students to work in groups to collaborate on something related to the lesson focus. In this part of the lesson, students' expectations are that they now start to fully utilize the proper academic language while working collaboratively to improve and consolidate their level of understanding in the application of the skill.

You Do

"You DO" implies this portion of the GRM requires students to independently apply their newly learnt skill. This is the time for the teacher to listen and observe in order to assess any deficiency and plan for any future intervention. This portion of the GRM should not be rushed as ample time is needed for students to practice the skill before they can apply it independently.

It should be noted there is no prescribed order to the GRM. Any portion of the GRM can be used in any order so long as all four portions are covered appropriately (Fisher & Frey, 2008a).

Wrap Up

While not technically part of the framework, many teachers include a final group wrap-up in the instructional process. This is a time for students to ask questions and share their new learnings. Perhaps most important, it is during this time the instructors and students celebrate the success of what has been learnt.

5E Defined

In contrast to the GRM, the 5E Model of Instruction is inquiry based and developed by Biological Sciences Curriculum Study, specifically for use in teaching science concepts, though its use has expanded through the years to include other concept-based categories of study (Bybee et, 2006). The components of the model include:

Engage

To capture students' interest and attention, as well as to elicit students' prior knowledge.

Explore

Students are provided with activities along with ample time and the opportunity for conceptual change in order to resolve the disequilibrium created within the engage portion of the lesson.

Explain

The teacher directs students' attention to the two previous phases and asks for their explanations of the phenomenon or concept under study. It is also here the teacher will counter any lingering misconceptions, often by redirecting students back to the data collected during the "Explore" portion. The teacher may also need to fill gaps not able to be covered within the "Explore" so students can start to construct their new understandings. Throughout this portion, the teacher is listening, observing, and guiding students, often with questioning, towards a more sophisticated scientific understanding of the concept. It should be noted in this portion of the lesson, this is not where the teacher conducts a lecture to explain the concept.

Elaborate

In this portion, the goal is to extend, expand, or enrich the concepts or abilities gained from the previous portions of the lesson. This is accomplished by bringing in relevancy to the concept, or expanding the knowledge to new situations, or even making links to other domains. This can be done through web-quests, additional text, web-based simulations, or engineering design challenges.

Evaluate

As all of us live within the age of accountability, assessment is not just important to guide future learning; it is an expectation by the institution we work within. That said, while the evaluate portion of the lesson appears last, it by no means implies assessment only occurs after instruction. As teachers, we realize we must constantly evaluate our students in order to support learners and gauge the success of the lesson.

Where Do These Models Go Off Course and Why?

The author has had much experience in seeing what actual practice looks like inside classrooms. The following are take-aways from decades of experience of doing observations in thousands of classrooms:

5E – Common Pitfalls in Practice

1. The explain portion turns into a lecture versus a discussion and presentation of student data.
2. Videos used in the "Engage" section may over, or fully, explain the concept. Too much explanation all at once will take away interest in the exploration. It also misses the point of the engage to elicit students'

prior pre or misconceptions of the concept, a critical component of conceptual change (Strike & Posner, 1985).

3. Teachers often provide too much information instead of asking leading or guiding questions.
4. "Explore" is done as a demonstration by the teacher. Instead, during this section, students should share an experience of inquiry that will later be discussed, clarified, and built upon.
5. Inquiry as a methodology is abandoned due to worries of covering content (Mehmet & Southerland, 2012).

GRM – Common Pitfalls in Instruction

1. Skipping from "I DO" (i.e., modelling) to "YOU DO" (i.e., independent practice). Students must have time to practice in a guided and supported manner. This can be quite problematic as students may take on a misconception that will take even more time to unlearn (Fisher and Frey, 2008).
2. Not utilizing probing questions to identify areas of weakness to provide the essential feedback students need to develop proficiency.
3. Not utilizing high level questioning techniques throughout lesson.
4. Listening to instructions on how to do a task versus experiencing how the teacher models the thinking process involved in the task.

Conclusions

It is apparent these two models share many attributes, namely they are both student-centered, based in constructivism, and designed to help students construct more sophisticated understandings. Both require students to be active participants in their own learning. The biggest differences lie in the purpose. The GRM is for the learning of skills and processes, while 5E is best suited for the learning of concepts as it is uniquely built to assist with ~~a~~ students' conceptual change. Both have great strengths and have withstood decades of research in their usage. Unfortunately, the use of these well-established models is not without problems. The GRM can too easily be converted into a positivist methodology where students sit passively, perhaps taking notes, only to be asked to mirror what the teacher has done rather than develop the skills necessary to become an independent learner.

The 5E Model is often abandoned for many of the same reasons as teachers are often reluctant to release the learning to the student via the inquiry practice. Of course, there is always the looming worry over time in this environment of accountability (Mehmet & Southerland, 2012). Whatever the reason for teachers not fully embracing or implementing these models, educational leaders will need to assist teachers to embrace not being the sole source of knowledge, acknowledging the need for a student-centered classroom, and becoming a constructivist at heart. Teachers also need assistance in gaining a better understanding of the true intentions and usage of these two student-centered and constructivist models.

References:

Bybee, R, & Taylor, J. & Gardner, A. & Scotter, P. & Carlson, J. & Westbrook, A. & Landes, N. (2006). The BSCS 5E Instructional Model: Origins, Effectiveness, and Applications. BSCS.

Driver, R. (1983). *The Pupil as Scientist?* Milton Keynes, UK: Open University Press.

Fisher, D., & Frey, N. (2008). Homework and the gradual release of responsibility: Making "responsibility" possible. English Journal, 98(2), 40-45.

Fisher, D., & Frey, N. (2008a). Better Learning Through Structured Teaching: A Framework for the Gradual Release of Responsibility. Alexandria, VA: Association for Supervision and Curriculum Development.

Mehmet, A. & Southerland, S. (2012). A National Survey of Middle and High School Science Teachers' Responses to Standardized Testing: Is Science Being Devalued in Schools? Journal of Science Teacher Education 23, 233–257 DOI 10.1007/s10972-012-9266-3

Moon, J.A. (1999). Reflection in Learning and Professional Development: Theory and Practice (1st ed.). Routledge. https://doi.org/10.4324/9780203822296

NASA. (2012). 5Es Overview: The 5E instructional model. Archived from the original on 23 September 2008. Retrieved May 27, 2021

Pearson, P.D.; Gallagher, M. (October 1983). "The Instruction of Reading Comprehension" (PDF). *Contemporary Educational Psychology*. Washington, DC: University of Illinois, National Institute of Education. 8 (3): 317–344. doi:10.1016/0361-476X(83)90019-X. hdl:2142/17939.

Piaget, J. & Inhelder, B. (1942). *The child's construction of quantities: conservation and atomism*. London: Routledge and Kegan Paul.

Strike, K. A., & Posner, G. J. (1985). A conceptual change view of learning and understanding. In L. West & L. Pines (Eds.), Cognitive structure and conceptual change (pp. 211–231). New York: Academic Press.

Vygotsky, L.S. (1978). Mind in Society: The Development of the Higher Psychological Processes. Cambridge, MA: The Harvard University Press. (Originally published 1930, New York: Oxford University Press.)

CHAPTER 12: QUESTIONING: A NECESSARY CURRENCY

In a world where accountability is a centerpiece in a data-driven educational system, instruction and assessment have evolved into two sides of the same coin. In the classroom, teachers ask questions both to help students think more deeply about content and to assess what and how they comprehend content that has been previously taught. In a typical classroom, a teacher may ask several hundred questions per day as part of their instructional practice, but what is the quality of those questions and how well are they posed?

Unfortunately, the ability to ask 'good' questions, or even the process of questioning is not easy. All too often, most questions posed by teachers are focused on memorization and recall. These types of questions are focused on a single right answer and not the types of questions that may encourage deeper student understandings of content (Mehan, 1979; Wilen, 1991). The lack of ability to ask good questions is not just limited to teacher candidates or new teachers. Even teachers with advanced degrees, including college professors are often not proficient at modeling best practices when it comes to questioning (Ciardiello, 1991). The question then becomes, why, and what do teachers need to know to be more proficient at asking good questions?

Types of Questions

A teacher candidate or new teacher must understand the types of questions, what are the benefits and pitfalls of each, as well as the best techniques for asking questions. To start, what is the purpose of asking questions? Certainly, questions help teachers assess what students know and how they know it, serving as both a quantitative and qualitative measuring stick for learning. They also provide opportunities for the social construction of knowledge by allowing students to vocalize their thoughts and listen to the views presented by their peers as they answer questions. There is also a crucial participation component that enable students to feel connected to the learning (Brualdi, 1998).

McComas & Abraham (2004) describes how questions can be differentiated into four quadrants (See Appendix A for descriptions). Questions can be a combination of higher or lower order and convergent or divergent (e.g., lower order-convergent, lower order divergent, higher order convergent, and higher order divergent). Lower order questions are centered on the recall of facts, such as names of scientists, dates of discovery, definitions, or identification of categories. Higher order questions require students to not just know facts, but to also understand the facts in relationship to a context. For example, instead of knowing the parts of a plant, a student understands how the parts of a plant work together to enable a plant to make its own food and even how this process distinguishes plants from animals. Now to compare divergent and convergent questions using the similar frame of reference. An example of a convergent question might be, why do some plants have brightly colored flowers? This convergent question measures a student's ability to understand the role of flowers and their coloration. A related divergent question might be: what might happen if the plant no longer produces brightly colored flowers? This divergent question attempts to examine a student's ability to extrapolate and provide a potential scenario for what may happen to the long-term propagation of the plant.

It is not that lower order questions are not important, as there must be a balance between lower and higher, divergent and convergent, questions. For example, convergent question's purpose is a test of factual knowledge. It is also useful for arousing student curiosity, and for setting the stage for higher-order questions yet to come (Musumeci, 1996). A teacher may also use these types of questions to start a series of questions. This practice can be effective when used with ELLs or ESE students in the class to help them feel included in the discourse (Shomoossi, 2004). Unfortunately, research shows that teachers all too often spend too much time emphasizing factual knowledge (Wilen, 1987), especially given that such knowledge is quickly forgotten (Sanders, 1966). It should be noted that students need more than just exposure to lower-level convergent types of questions to develop the critical thinking skills the educational community hopes for (Tan, 2007).

In contrast, divergent questions, force students to think critically by forcing them to synthesize and evaluate information. Therefore, it requires students to move beyond simple recall towards the necessitation of manipulating information and the construction of conclusions based on evidence (Gall, 1970). By posing cognitively elevated questions may not guarantee higher-order thinking, but it does grant the best chance (Black et al., 2003). Given the knowledge of what types of questions to ask, the next question would be, when does questioning apply in a science classroom?

Strategies for Questioning

While asking higher-order questions should be the goal, it may not be the starting point. Posing a higher-order question from the start may result in a lot of blank stares from students. Like any type of learning, questions need to be purposefully scaffolded, with the questions adapted to meet the needs of the individual students being called upon to answer. These adaptations of questions may be based on language or ability levels of the individual student.

It is also important to create an environment that students feel safe answering, even if they end up not being 'correct.' The concept of 'not being correct' may be something many students fear based upon their past experiences. The teacher can help to set the tone for these types of discussions by promoting the idea that classroom dialogue involves learning, not testing. Of course, some students still may have excessive anxiety about voicing what they know in front of their peers, therefore, it should be acceptable for students to take a pass on a question and allowed to re-enter the discussion when they are ready. Remind students that engaging in dialogue is also vital practice for the development of public speaking skills.

Another critical aspect of good questioning is accomplished by not giving answers. Once the teacher acknowledges, or rejects, an answer, students may lose interest resulting in a decrease of future learning opportunities (Black & Wiliam, 1998; Leung & Mohan, 2004). One technique to use is when students provide an answer, a teacher may probe more deeply having the students complete, clarify, expand, or support their answers with evidence. A teacher can also continue this same line of questioning by asking other students to add on or voice opposing viewpoints. By doing so, a single question can reach greater depths and have a more natural conversational flow than a long series of short individual questions. It can also encourage more peer-to-peer discussion to the point students may start to ask their own questions. In these cases, if the question is directed toward the teacher, it is a good practice to redirect the question back to the class.

"Wait time," often called "think time," is another critical aspect of good questioning techniques. Wait time is when a teacher pauses after posing a question to allow time for all students to process the question and develop a coherent answer. The time for this pause may be 3-5 seconds, just enough for processing to occur. After the student answers the question, the teacher should again pause before proceeding. While it sounds easy, not talking and allowing silence to fill the classroom can be uncomfortable and unnatural. Research tells us that most instructors only wait between 0.7 seconds and 1.4 seconds with the lower end of the timeframe more common when the teacher believes students do not know the answer to the posed question (Rowe, 1972). On the brighter side, the same research also noted that when 'think time' is appropriately applied, students were more successful at answering the posed questions.

Conclusions

During a typical day, a teacher may ask questions during 80% of the day, which amounts to approximately 300-400 questions (Leven & Long, 1981). Unfortunately, 95% of the questions asked by teachers require only a short answer based on recall rather than forcing a deeper reflection by the student (Wilen, 1991). For this reason, it would seem vital that teacher candidates and new teachers gain the skills necessary to utilize the best practices of questioning, especially considering its importance as a key formative assessment strategy to promote learning. Using questioning, teachers can gain insight into student's understandings of content, as well as interpret that information gathered to make more effective decisions about future instruction (Black et al., 2003; Jiang, 2014). Asking good questions is an essential skill required by effective teachers as questioning transcends both instructions and assessment, thereby confirming it as a valuable currency.

References:

Black, P., Harrison, C., Lee, C., Marshall, B., and Wiliam, D. (2003). *Assessment for Learning: Putting it Into Practice*. Buckingham: Open University Press.

Black, P., & Wiliam, D. (1998). *Inside the Black Box: Raising Standards Through Classroom Assessment.* London: King's College London School of Education.

Brualdi, Amy C. (1998). *Classroom questions*. ERIC Clearinghouse on Assessment and Evaluation, Washington DC.

Carless, D. (2011). *From Testing to Productive Student Learning: Implementing Formative Assessment in Confucian-Heritage Settings*. New York, NY: Routledge.

Ciardiello, Angelo, V. (1998). Did you ask a good question today? Alternative cognitive and metacognitive strategies. *Journal of Adolescent & Adult Literacy*, 42(3), 210-219.

Gall, M. D. (1970). The use of questions in teaching. *Rev. Educ. Res.* 44, 707–721. doi: 10.3102/00346543040005707

Hu, Q., Nicholson, A., & Chen, W. (2004). A survey on the questioning pattern of college English teachers. *For. Lang. World* 6, 22–27.

Jackson, J. (2002). Reticence in second language case discussions: anxiety and aspirations. *System* 30, 65–84. doi: 10.1016/S0346-251X (01)00051-3

Leung, C., &d Mohan, B. (2004). Teacher formative assessment and talk in classroom context: assessment as discourse and assessment of discourse. *Lang. Test.* 21, 335–359. doi: 10.1191/0265532204lt287oa

Leven, T. and Long, R. (1981). *Effective instruction*. Washington DC: Association for Supervision and Curriculum Development.

McComas, W., & Abraham, L. (2004). Asking More Effective Questions. Los Angeles: Rossier School of Education.

Mehan, H. (1979). *Learning Lessons: Social Organization in the Classroom.* Cambridge, MA: Harvard University Press.

Musumeci, D. (1996). Teacher-learner negotiation in content-based instruction: communication at cross-purposes? *Appl. Linguist.* 17, 286–325. doi: 10.1093/applin/17.3.286

Peng, J. E. (2012). Towards an ecological understanding of willingness to communicate in EFL classrooms in China. *System* 40, 203–213. doi: 10.1016/j.system.2012.02.002

Ross, W. (1860). Methods of instruction. *Barnard's American Journal of Education 9*, 367-79.

Sanders, N. M. (1966). *Classroom Questions: What Kinds?* New York, NY: Harper and Row.

Shomoossi, N. (2004). The effect of teachers' questioning behavior on EFL classroom interaction: a classroom research study. *Read. Matrix* 4, 96–104.

Smith, F., Hardman, F., Wall, K., & Mroz, M. (2004). Interactive whole class teaching in the national literacy and numeracy strategies. *Br. Educ. Res. J.* 30, 395–411. doi: 10.1080/01411920410001689706

Tan, Z. (2007). Questioning in Chinese university EL classrooms: what lies beyond it? *RELC J.* 38, 87–103. doi: 10.1177/0033688206076161

Wilen, William W. (1991). *Questioning Skills for Teachers,* third edition. National Education Association, Washington DC.

CHAPTER 13: PEDAGOGY AND BELIEF SYSTEMS

At the core of educational experiences is the desire for students to construct sophisticated understandings of content, and not just absorb simple content knowledge through rote memorization. This development of more complex forms of thought about the world requires qualitative changes in reasoning. As a result, school districts have spent enormous amounts of money on training science teachers to be more effective in the classroom by improving their "teaching skills and content knowledge." Accountability systems have also been put in place to encourage teachers to perform better, measured by the outcomes of their students on standardized tests. With the tremendous commitment toward improvement, why is there so little change in student scores? According to NAEP (2019), the overall trend for science scores has remained mostly flat over the past decade. It is also true that many teachers have a deficit when it comes to content knowledge (Lederman, 1992). Perhaps these teachers lacking in content knowledge also need a more sustained approached at utilizing "best practices?" Both prior reasons could be true, but even if they were both put in place, would instruction dramatically change? Could it be that the focus has been misplaced and the issue is seated deeply within a teacher's very own beliefs about knowledge and knowledge construction?

Epistemological beliefs: teacher's beliefs about the nature of knowledge and knowing.

Many who have progressed this far in their educational journey have heard terms such as student-centered versus teacher-centered classrooms. You may have also heard how students are not empty vessels in which knowledge can be poured. In either case, what does this all mean for classroom practices? As it turns out, quite a lot. Teacher beliefs about knowledge and knowledge construction are the major predictor of the type of practice that will occur in the classroom. Research has demonstrated (Tsai, 2002, 2007; Yang et al., 2008) that a teacher's beliefs about how knowledge is constructed (i.e., their epistemological beliefs), can be at odds with constructivist student-centered teaching practices.

Positivism and Constructivism

What can be thought of as student-centered, has its roots in constructivism, which is the basis for modern teacher reform movements. Constructivism is where knowledge is something the learner creates or constructs and not something passed from omniscient authority to the naive passive learner (Feucht & Bendixen, 2010). These constructivist epistemological beliefs are important because these ideals are necessary to drive the type of instruction called for in reforms and reflective of the type of instruction necessary for the development of a student's sophisticated understandings of content.

Unfortunately, the practice of science teaching has succumbed to teachers' beliefs that conflict with constructivism (Tsai, 2002). As suggested by Yang et al., these opposing beliefs to constructivism suggest positions that are "philosophically more like that of the positivist" (2008, p.13). Positivism is a contrasting view of how knowledge is created. Within a positivist methodology, practice shifts from the student-centered to the teacher-centered perspective, where knowledge is given and not constructed, and the teacher becomes the omniscient authority and the holder of knowledge. Cohen (1990), and more recently, Tsai (2006), suggest the root of the problem can be found in a teachers' deep-rooted transmission beliefs. These epistemological beliefs associated with transmission of knowledge leads to a shift towards more lecture, rote-learning, and cookbook labs. In other words, a teacher's beliefs about knowledge and knowledge construction can be at loggerheads with the promoted reform-minded philosophies associated with learning (Tsai, 2002). If teachers have a view centered in positivism, is it any wonder why difficulty arises as they attempt to teach using reform-minded instructional techniques of constructivism that are most beneficial to students?

The learning theory of constructivism comes directly out of the work of Piaget and Vygotsky (Slavin, 2000), though its influence can be traced back to the social pedagogical ideas of the educational philosophers Rousseau, Pestalozzi, and Fröbel (Kornbeck & Jensen, 2009). Perhaps most well-known in American education is the work of Dewey in the early part of the 20th century. It was Dewey who put focus on the learner with his student-centered approach of education and who stated that "education is a constant reorganization or reconstructing of experience" (Dewey, 1916/1966, p. 89). More than a century since Dewey, while his ideas are commonplace within the halls of academia and modern learning theories, the true practice of constructivist teaching methods are unfortunately observed on a much lesser degree, but why?

Research tells us that an individual teacher's beliefs concerning knowledge and knowledge construction, either implicit or explicit, are a more predictive factor in determining the types of instructional practices implemented in the classroom than either content knowledge or knowledge of instructional strategies (Jones & Carter, 2007; Pajares, 1992, Tsai, 2002, 2006). Perhaps the most critical point to make given the current state of accountability within education is that a teachers' beliefs are a principal factor in determining student outcomes (Hofer & Pintrich, 2002; Pajares, 1992; Schraw & Olafson, 2002), making the case for a new focus.

It would make sense that if the goal were to improve the overall stock of science teachers, a greater importance should be placed on developing and shaping teachers' personal epistemological beliefs. Given that epistemological beliefs, especially considering they are a more predictive factor in determining the types of instructional practices than either content knowledge or learned instructional strategies (Jones & Carter, 2007; Pajares, 1992; Richardson, 1996) need to be emphasized. Other research reports (Fenstermacher & Richardson, 2000) that good teaching within many pedagogical paradigms is synonymous with constructivist teaching. It is not to say a positivist style of teaching is ineffective, only that instructional methods must be aligned to instructional goals (Kuhn, 2007). In short, if teachers have beliefs that are not associated with constructivism, they will struggle to teach science well. This is especially troublesome given that the very nature of science is about constructing scientific knowledge.

Conclusions

In conclusion, the problem is not that these teachers cannot be taught "How to Teach" or to learn the "Best Practices;" rather, it is that these teachers may be encumbered by their personal epistemological perspectives rooted in positivism and are not able to teach in an appropriate and most effective manner. They are held back philosophically by their own personal epistemological beliefs and as a result, so are their students. As intentions to teach using the most effective practices are a crucial factor in the teaching, then a transformation of teachers' epistemological beliefs must take place, as these values are what shape classroom behaviors (Bell and Pearson, 1992). Therefore, it would seem prudent that if the science education community expects changes to occur in student understandings of science, science education must first realize that the teachers' content knowledge and knowledge of best practices may not be the largest problem. For authentic change to occur, then a concerted effort towards recasting teachers in a constructivist light is in order.

References:

Bell, B. F., & Pearson, J. (1992). Better learning. *International Journal of Science Education*, 14(3), 349-361.

Cohen, A. D. (1990). *Language learning: Insights for learners, instructors, and researchers*. New York: Newbury House/HarperCollins.

Dewey, J. (1933). *How we think*. Buffalo, NY: Prometheus Books (Original work published 1910).

Dewey, J. (1966/1916). *Democracy and Education. An introduction to the philosophy of education* (1916 edn). New York: Free Press.

Fenstermacher, G. D., & Richardson, V. (2000). On Making Determinations of Quality in Teaching. Paper commissioned by the *Board on International Comparative Studies in Education of the National Academies/National Research Council*.

Feucht, F., & Bendixen, L. D. (2010). Personal epistemology in the classroom: A welcome and guide for the reader. In L. Bendixen, & F. Feucht, (Eds). *Personal Epistemology in the Classroom* (pp. 3-28). New York: Cambridge University Press.

Hofer, B., & Pintrich, P. (1997). The development of epistemological theories: Beliefs about knowledge and knowing and their relation to learning. *Review of Educational Research*, 67, 88-140.

Jones, M. G., & Carter, G. (2007). Science teacher attitudes and beliefs. In S. Abell, & N. Lederman, (Eds.), *Handbook of research on science education* (pp. 1067- 1104). Mahwah, New Jersey: Lawrence Erlbaum Associates.

Kornbeck, J. & Rosendal Jensen, N. (2009) 'Introduction: Social pedagogy in Europe – diverse with common features', in Kornbeck, J. and Rosendal Jensen, N. (eds), *The diversity of social pedagogy in Europe*, Bremen, Europäischer Hochschulverlag.

Kuhn, D. (2007). Is direct instruction an answer to the right question? *Educational Psychologist*, 42(2), 109–113.

Lederman, N. (1992). Students' and teachers' conceptions of the nature of science: A review of the research. *Journal of Research in Science Teaching*, 29, 331-359.

National Assessment of Education Progress (2019). Science Framework for the 2015 National Assessment of Educational Progress. National Assessment Governing Board, U.S. Department of Education. Retrieved from https://www.nationsreportcard.gov/science/?grade=12 on October, 17, 2021

Olafson, L., & Shraw, G. (2010). Beyond epistemology: assessing teachers' epistemological and ontological worldviews. In L. Bendixen, & F. Feucht, (Eds.), *Personal Epistemology in the Classroom* (pp. 516-552). New York: Cambridge University Press.

Pajares, M. F. (1992). Teachers' beliefs and educational research: cleaning up a messy construct. *Review of Educational Research*, 62(3), 307-332.

Richardson, V. (1996). The role of attitudes and beliefs in learning to teach. In J. Sikula, (Eds.), *The handbook of research in teacher education* (2nd ed., pp. 102-119). New York: Macmillan.

Schraw, G., & Olafson, L. (2002). Teacher's epistemological worldviews and educational practices. *Issues in Education*, 8(2), 99-148.

Slavin, R. (2000). *Educational Psychology*. 6th ed. Boston: Allyn and Bacon

Tsai, C. C. (2002). Nested epistemologies: Science teachers' beliefs of teaching, learning and science. *International Journal of Science Education*, 24, 771-783.

Tsai, C. C. (2006). Reinterpreting and reconstructing science: Teachers' view changes toward the nature of science by courses of science education. *Teaching & Teacher Education*, 22, 363 – 375.

Tsai, C. C. (2007). Teachers' scientific epistemological views: The coherence with instruction and students' views. *Science Education*, 91, 222-43.

Yang, F., Chang, C. Y., & Hsu, Y. S. (2008). Teacher views about constructivist instruction and personal epistemology: a national study in Taiwan. *Educational Studies*, 34(5), 527 - 542.

CHAPTER 14: OVERCOMING STUDENT MISCONCEPTIONS

Does gravity effect heavier objects more than lighter objects? Will gravity cause heavy objects to fall faster than lighter objects? When you back up from a mirror, do you see more of yourself? Is there gravity in space? These are all interesting questions that seem intuitive, but are they? We think about science as observations of the natural world, so it makes sense that if we have made observations within our daily lives, we would know science, but is that a safe assumption? For example, we may watch astronauts floating while aboard the International Space Station (ISS), therefore, it is easy to make a claim about the non-existence of gravity based on that one observation. Unfortunately, that is not a correct conclusion. In fact, the gravitational force acting on the ISS is roughly 90% of what is felt on Earth's surface, so how can astronauts appear to float? The actual reason astronauts aboard the ISS appear to float is due to its orbit around Earth resulting in what is referred to as 'Apparent Weightlessness,' and not actual weightlessness. People tend to have many misconceptions about common everyday phenomena, so what does that mean for teaching science?

Types of Misconceptions

Misconceptions in science are those commonly held beliefs that have no basis in actual scientific fact. The National Research Council (1997) describes 5 types of misconceptions listed below:

- *Preconceived notions* - views rooted in everyday experiences (e.g., gravity effects heavy objects more than light objects).
- *Nonscientific beliefs* – views learned from other sources other than science education, such as religious or mythical teachings.
- *Conceptual misunderstandings* - Views that are derived from previous instruction, such as when science is presented as a set of facts and where students are not forced to confront paradoxes or their own preconceived notions (e.g., astronauts appear to float but gravity holds the Moon in orbit about the Earth).
- *Vernacular misconceptions* – views that arise from terminology where they have one meaning within the scientific community and another in everyday language (e.g., work & theory).
- *Factual misconceptions* - views resulting from past learning, often learned in childhood that carry forward into adulthood (e.g., lightning never strikes the same place twice)

Though there are multiple types of potential students' misconceptions to deal with, they are also not created equal when it comes to eliminating them.

Conceptual Change & The 5E Model for Instruction

Primarily, the vernacular and factual misconceptions are often easily tackled through simple discussion. Students may even self-correct as they are exposed to content (NRC, 1997). Unfortunately, tackling students preconceived notions or deeply rooted nonscientific beliefs is more of a challenge.

It must be kept in mind it is not the job of a science educator to replace religious beliefs, but it is our job to help students understand how the process of science creates knowledge using a specific set of methods (i.e., the methods of science). In these situations, the hope is students will understand the concept and how the conclusions were made, but not necessarily believe them. In other words, science education stays in their own lane and allows the students to develop an understanding, albeit compartmentalize from their personal beliefs. According to the NRC, (1997, p.28) "it is not effective for a teacher simply to insist that the learner dismiss preconceived notions and ingrained nonscientific beliefs." Making distinctions between scientific knowledge (i.e., knowledge gained empirically) and personal (often religious) beliefs can be complex and confusing for both students and teachers. As teachers of science, our goal needs to focus on changing students' knowledge about science concepts and how those understandings were constructed, not student's personally held beliefs (Southerland, Sinatra, & Matthews, 2001).

Research into conceptual change tells us is that new concepts cannot be learned if misconceptions about the concept are presently deep-rooted in the mind of the student. In such cases, the student's existing, often simplistic, model of reality allows them to make sense of their environment. This situation makes the adoption of a more scientifically sound and often more complex conception more difficult (Mayer, 1987). It is important that educators understand that if students hold onto these misconceptions, it can hinder future learning (McDermott, 1991). So, how can educators help students overcome their misconceptions? Before any success is possible of transforming student concepts, students must first acknowledge and confront their prior conceptions through a conceptual change process.

Perhaps the best known of these models explaining the process was developed by Posner, Strike, Hewson, and Gertzog (1982) for use in a classroom setting. The model explicitly explains the student's cognitive shifts during instruction in their understandings of a concept. Theorists and educational researchers (Chi et al., 1994; Dial et al., 2009; Ebert & Crippen, 2010; McLeod, 2015; Vosniadou et al., 2011) argue that students use mental frameworks to organize information to help them make sense of the natural world. By gaining more information through learning, the student must somehow add additional information to the existing knowledge. If this added information gained runs counter to existing knowledge, a process of conceptual change must be undertaken to assimilate this new knowledge into the mental framework. (Hewson, 1992; Posner et al., 1982). Posner et.al. (1982) suggests that classical conceptual change is similar to the Kuhn's (1970) notion of a paradigm shift and Piaget's (Wadsworth, 2004) notion of assimilation, accommodation, and disequilibrium. The mental model for conceptual change suggests that students progress through a series of steps on their way to assimilating and accommodation a new conception more aligned to the views of the scientific community.

These steps include (Stepans, 2003):

- Eliciting students' preconceptions and misconceptions
- Confront students existing ideas through scientific investigations
- Accommodating the conceptual shift toward new views through discussion and debate
- Extend and potentially solidify the new understanding by providing opportunities for students to expand upon and apply their new knowledge in novel settings

Fortunately for science teachers, there are methods that are well designed to help students uncover, confront, and provide opportunities to interact with new knowledge. Inquiry, and specifically the 5E Instructional Model (Bybee, 2006) provides such a tool. The 5 stages of the 5E instructional model design provides a mechanism to allow students to experience conceptual change via the inquiry process. However, research tells us that for conceptual change to take place, teachers must explicitly target misconceptions within a lesson (Posner, et. al., 1982). But is it a certainty that teachers know and understand the common student misconceptions?

Teacher Content Knowledge as a Factor

Few would deny that teachers of science need some level of content knowledge to be proficient, but what does having content knowledge truly mean? Should teachers have deep knowledge of the subject matter they are teaching, gleaned from undergraduate studies, additional graduate courses, or even research experience? Is there some optimal combination of these different types of knowledge or is it more complicated than that? Could the actual key to increasing academic achievement be held in a teacher's knowledge of common student misconceptions as some researchers have long suggested (Ausubel, Novak, & Hanesian, 1978)?

More recently, researchers now suggest that teachers need to have knowledge of the common student misconceptions that are encountered within a course (Carlsen, 1999; Loughran, Berry, & Mulhall, 2012). More recent research describes how a teacher's knowledge of student common misconceptions are more impactful for student achievement than teachers having some amount of content knowledge and viewing science only as a set of facts or as a set of scientific truths. Therefore, a teachers' subject-matter knowledge may be deemed requisite but is not a sufficient precondition to help students replace their misconceptions with conceptions more inline of the science education community (Sadler & Sonnet, 2016).

Conclusions

In the quest to improve students' understandings of and about science, misconceptions can be a tremendous barrier. Research informs us that students deeply rooted misconceptions can hinder future learning (McDermott, 1991). Therefore, it is vital that students are taught in a way they can replace their original conceptions with those more accurate conceptions through a process called, 'conceptual change.'

For students to improve their understanding of concepts, teachers must first, as a prerequisite have an adequate subject matter knowledge. Beyond knowledge of science content, teachers must also have knowledge of common student misconceptions held within the content to be taught (Carlsen, 1999; Loughran, Berry, & Mulhall, 2012, Sadler & Sonnet, 2016). They must also understand the process necessary for conceptual change to take place, plus a mechanism by which to implement conceptual change through. Fortunately, science teachers may rely on familiar instructional models. And from there, it is a matter of knowing the common misconceptions held by students and then explicitly targeting them. With these conditions met, students have the potential to academically thrive.

References:

Bybee, R, & Taylor, J. & Gardner, A. & Scotter, P. & Carlson, J. & Westbrook, A. & Landes, N. (2006). The BSCS 5E Instructional Model: Origins, Effectiveness, and Applications. BSCS.

Chi, M. T. H., Slotta, J. D., and de Leeuw, N. (1994). From Things to Process: A Theory of Conceptual Change for Learning Science Concepts. Learning and Instruction 4: 27-43.

David P. Ausubel, Joseph D. Novak, and Helen Hanesian, (1978). *Educational Psychology: A Cognitive View*, 2nd ed. (New York: Holt, Rinehart, and Winston, 1978).

Dial, K., Riddley, D., Williams, K., and Sampson, V. (2009). Addressing Misconceptions: a demonstration to help students understand the law of conservation of mass. *The Science Teacher* 76(7): 54-57.

Ebert, E. K., and Crippen, K. J. (2010). Applying a Cognitive-Affective Model of Conceptual Change to Professional Development. *Journal of Science Teacher Education* 21: 371–388.

Heather C. Hill, Stephen G. Schilling, and Deborah Loewenberg Ball (2004). Developing Measures of Teachers' Mathematics Knowledge for Teaching, *Elementary School Journal* 105: 11–30.

Hewson, Peter W., and N. Richard Thorley. (1989). "The conditions of conceptual change in the classroom." *International Journal of Science Education* 11.5: 541-553.

John Loughran, Amanda Berry, and Pamela Mulhall (2012). *Understanding and Developing Science Teachers' Pedagogical Content Knowledge*, 2nd ed. Rotterdam: Sense Publishers

Kuhn T. S. (1970) *"The Structure of Scientific Revolutions"*, Chicago, Chicago University Press.

Lee S. Shulman, (1986). Those Who Understand: Knowledge Growth in Teaching, *Educational Researcher* 15, no. 2: 4–14.

McLeod, S. A. (2015). Jean Piaget - Cognitive Theory. Retrieved from www.simplypsychology.org/piaget.html

National Research Council. 1997. *Science Teaching Reconsidered: A Handbook*. Washington, DC: The National Academies Press.https://doi.org/10.17226/5287.

Pamela L. Grossman (1990). *The Making of a Teacher: Teacher Knowledge and Teacher Education.* New York: Teachers College Press.

Posner, G. J., Strike, K. A., Hewson, P. W., & Gertzog, W. A. (1982). "Accommodation of a scientific conception: Towards a theory of conceptual change," *Science Education*, vol. 66, no.2, pp. 211-227

Sadler, P. and Sonnert, G. (2016). Understanding Misconceptions: Teaching and Learning in Middle School Physical Science. *American Educator, spring 2016 edition.*

Southerland, Sherry & Sinatra, Gale & Matthews, Michael. (2001). Belief, Knowledge, and Science Education. Educational Psychology Review. 13. 10.1023/A:1011913813847.

Stepans, J. (2003). *Targeting Students' Science Misconceptions: Physical Science Concepts Using the Conceptual Change Model*. Riverview, FL: Idea Factory.

Vosniadou, S., Ioannides, C., Dimitrakopoulou, A., & Papademetriou, E. (2011). Designing learning environments to promote conceptual change in science. *Learning and Instruction* 11: 381–419.

William S. Carlsen (1999). “Domains of Teacher Knowledge,” in Examining Pedagogical Content Knowledge: The Construct and Its Implications for Science Education, ed. Julie Gess-Newsome and Norman G. Lederman (Boston: Kluwer Academic, 1999), 133–144.

Wadsworth, B. J. (2004). *Piaget's theory of cognitive and affective development: Foundations of constructivism*. New York: Longman.

CHAPTER 15: SCIENCE AND ASSESSMENT

It would seem obvious that a teacher needs to determine what a student already knows, how well they are learning, how much they are learning, and the quality of that learning. To be able to gather this information a teacher must assess their students. In education, the term *assessment* describes the process used to gather information to measure and evaluate data on students' knowledge and skills to better align instruction to student achievement. But while typically it is thought assessment targets students, who else and what else is being assessed in this process?

The art of teaching can be compared to sailing a ship. A destination may be known, a course charted, but continuous evaluations of the environment may require many ongoing adjustments to sails and rudder. In the classroom environment, it is data derived from assessments that helps the teacher make the necessary course adjustments regarding instruction.

The Teacher and Classroom Assessments

The three basic types of assessments commonly used by science teachers in their practice to evaluate students are as follows:

- *Diagnostic Assessment* - used to determine the current content knowledge and understanding a student has. Typically done prior to the start of instruction to better determine individual students' strengths and weaknesses with content.
- *Formative Assessment* - Used to support on-going instruction. This assessment makes use of normal classroom activities and evaluates student knowledge throughout the lesson to determine potential future changes of a teacher's instructional practices
- *Summative Assessment* – used to determine what a student has learned after instruction.

Diagnostics

Diagnostic tests are perhaps the least familiar evaluation method for science teachers. Our counterparts in English Language Arts utilize diagnostics to determine a student's Reading Comprehension, Vocabulary, Fluency. and Decoding ability. One common use of a diagnostics in science classrooms is to determine which areas a student may require remediation before taking a high-stakes test. These diagnostics may be given a month before a EOC or other high stakes test to plan a more individualized learning plan. The tests are constructed to provide information about material from not just the current year, but previous years that are often covered on many State exams. By using the data from the diagnostic, a specific plan can be developed so a student focuses only on specific areas of weaknesses. Though we often think of a diagnostic as a more formal paper-pencil task, they can be done by making informal observation, through discussion, or examining student artifacts, etc. While diagnostics are used before instruction*, their design is often to help narrow the focus of instruction toward what a student does not know. Thereby, diagnostics are slightly different from a pre-test used in conjunction with a summative assessment to determine learning gains.

Formative Assessments

A formative assessment is used to evaluate on-going instruction. A formative assessment needs to be a well-planned process used to gather evidence about the current status of students' understandings regarding a concept or skill. These are done to assess a student's progress during the instruction, so instruction can be better tailored to the needs of the students. Students recognize formative assessments as short quizzes used as a check for understanding, the creation of concept maps to gauge the qualitative aspects of student understandings of concepts, or even quick polls of the classroom. These types of assessment can often pass without notice for a student who assumes that is just part of the lesson, but for a teacher this is where critical information is derived to evaluate student knowledge and needs. While it is possible to use some formatives for grading purpose, the use of formative assessments is much more effective when separated from the grading process altogether and used for the sole purpose of aiding instruction (Bloom 1969, p.48).

Summative Assessments

Teachers often think of summative assessments as those multiple-choice tests at the end of a unit or course. However, other types of assessments may be summative in nature, such as performance assessments and student presentations. Summative assessments typically occur at the conclusion of instruction, whether that be of a lesson, unit, or course. Summative assessments are often high stakes, which means that they have a high point value. Formatives tend to have low point value and are used as an incentive to complete the task. Examples of summative assessments include: a midterm exam, a final project, a paper, or a senior recital.

Progress Monitoring – A Fallacy?

Progress monitoring is a type of formative assessment and a common phrase heard in schools. In the K12 environment, progress monitoring refers to a set of written knowledge assessments given longitudinally across a school year (usually three to four times per year). This assessment type provides information about student's academic progress across time. Progress monitoring is often preferred over the solitary end-of-year or end-of-course methods. Multiple assessments make it possible to provide interventions or changes to instruction in a timely manner.

Progress monitoring can be highly effective at measuring the rate at which students are developing a specific content or skill, such as reading fluency. Unfortunately, progress monitoring does not work in heterogeneous disciplines. In most elementary science programs, different concepts are to be learned throughout the school year or even multiple years. Unlike the skill of reading that can be measured month over month or even year over year, science is not a singular skill or homogeneous content. Instead, science is a set of mostly discrete concepts. So, why is there a problem if the concepts to be learned are mostly discrete?

A typical science progression may have students learning about properties of matter the first nine weeks and interdependence of plants and animals the next. A learning gain over time only works if you are measuring the same thing. The point is, be very weary of the term 'progress monitoring' used in the same sentence as science.

Assessments in Science

In the science classroom, students should be learning through inquiry. The question becomes, what does assessment look like in a science classroom that is inquiry based? A common question administrators will ask teachers, "How do you know what students know?" Unlike many other disciplines, science is not a set of factoids acquired in an accretive manner or even a set of skills to be mastered. The learning of science involves conceptual change making it more difficult to provide the types of minute-by-minute quantitative data most are used to. Certainly, there can be the end of unit M/C assessment, but what about during instruction. How can a teacher know not just what students know, but more importantly, how they know it?

One of the best ways to ascertain what and how students know is by listening while students talk. This can be done more formally through short interviews and graded using a rubric. However, this information is often gained while students are engaged in the inquiry process. For example, while students are engaged in a hands-on activity, the teacher must do more than monitor for discipline or engagement with the task. As the teacher moves around the classroom and listens to student conversations, they may ask specific questions to groups or individual students. A clipboard can be carried to record the data on students' understandings. It may be a simple as a checkmark denoting if a student is currently below, on target, or above the learning goal. The same process can be used during discussion and/or presentations to ensure the quality of student understanding. This evaluation can provide critical information of which students may need intervention. It may also be a way to inform administrators about students' levels of understanding.

Conclusions

Teachers are responsible for providing the best possible instruction to their students. To do so they need to measure their effectiveness by assessing what and how students are learning. Fortunately, they have a set of tools at their disposal such as diagnostics, formatives, and summative assessment. Using the available assessment tools, teachers set goals for their instruction, they create the curriculum, they constantly take measurements to make sure they are on course. With skill, knowledge, and a willingness to encourage students to accompany you on this journey, both teacher and students can reach their goal.

References:

Bloom, B. S. (1969). Some theoretical issues relating to educational evaluation. In R. W. Tyler (Ed.), *Educational evaluation: new roles, new means*: the 63rd yearbook of the National Society for the Study of Education (part II) (Vol. 69(2), pp. 26-50). Chicago, IL: University of Chicago Press.

CHAPTER 16: EDUCATION REFORM

It is difficult to have a conversation about education these days without the dialogue veering into a discussion of standards and testing. It is not by chance these two topics are drawn together out of necessity. Questions about what students are being taught in school is certainly a valid concern, but what about the larger criticism about the need to get rid of standards themselves. There is also criticism of too much testing, but at the same time there are concerns about teachers and school's accountability. It would seem difficult to divorce them from one another.

Educational standards can be defined as the knowledge and skills students should attain due to instruction. Standards serve as the foundation of an accountability education system where clear and concise outcomes are needed to measure student success (National Research Council, 2001). To meet these demands, states have developed learning standards by grade level that are to be met by each student. Assessments are then created to measure to what extent students can demonstrate proficiency or learning gains on these standards, often in the case of End of Course (EOC) or End of Year (EOY) assessments. Students' scores on tests can be used to determine, promotion, future course placement, and even graduation in some cases if certain requirements are not satisfied.

Teachers and school administration are also measured using high-stakes assessments. A high- stakes assessment can be defined as any test that has major consequences. For example, standardized tests may be used to determine a school's grade as a report of adequacy. Standardized test may even provide a measure used to disperse monetary funds. They also serve as an important indicator to determine consequences for low performing schools (Elmore et al. 1996; Furman & Elmore 2004). Learning gains, as a measure of student improvement throughout the year, is commonly used in teacher evaluation rubrics. Teachers not performing to an appropriate level may be forced to move to an untested grade level. These teacher movements can also cause teachers to be moved to other schools. Then, teachers deemed more proficient may occupy positions that are to be tested using standardized state measures.

Rationale for Accountability

To provide a theoretical framework for the increases in assessment that is now very well known to students, teachers, administrators and parents, there are four major theories that support the current accountability environment:

- *Motivational Theory* – The notion that assessment is an extrinsic motivator for both student and teachers, thereby increasing academic achievement for students and the desire to improve teaching methods for teachers.
- *Alignment Theory* – The idea that the alignment of standards, curriculum, and assessments will provide a synergy within the educational system to increase outcomes.
- *Information Theory* – The belief that data provides critical information so that teachers and administrators can make informed decisions about instruction and curriculum.
- *Symbolism* – The understanding that accountability is a way to provide evidence the educational system is being responsible in its efforts to increase the academic success of students.

Although high-stakes or standardized test remain contentious, research does support the fact that many studies credit NCLB for raising academic performance in some disciplines, such as mathematics (Dee & Jacob, 2010). A caveat to this research suggests that it may not be the tests accountability that promotes better instruction, but instead, a realignment and narrowing of curriculum to the test may be the actual cause of gains. Unfortunately, the realignment and narrowing of focus has increased attention on some subjects such as mathematics and reading, while drastically reducing it in others (e.g., science & social studies) (Koretz, 2008; Renter et al., 2006; Rothstein, Jacobsen, & Wilder, 2008). While this is the current situation in education, it is important to know where this all started.

The History of Accountability

In 1983, a report from the National Commission on Excellence in Education issued a report entitled *A Nation at Risk*. The report detailed how the U.S. Education was failing to keep pace with its global competitors. The report cited diminishing SAT scores and comparisons with other developed nations as proof of a failing educational system. As history has proven, the report became a watershed event for education, not just in the U.S. but worldwide. It was from this one report from which a new wave of educational reforms was touched off and arguably equaling those following the launch of Sputnik. No area was untouched by this reform, as its reach encompassed not just national reforms, but state and local as well.

What resulted was a new theory in which to frame our educational system, outcome-based education (Spady, 1994). Outcome-based education (OBE) is based on the principle that the educational system should be based on a set of goals, or outcomes. Unlike some reform movements that promote specific instructional methods, OBE focuses on the alignment between coursework, student opportunities within the courses, and the eventual assessments to measure success towards the established goal(s) (Spady, 1994). The goal is that by the end of a student's educational experience, they will have met the established goals deemed appropriate to improve the Nation's status with regards to education.

In 1989, an educational summit that included George Bush along with the fifty state governors led to the adoption of set of national education goals to be reached by the year 2000, aptly entitled Goals 2000. Many of these goals were based upon the principle of OBE. In 1994, the Educate America Act was signed into law by then President Bill Clinton, which reauthorized the Elementary and Secondary Education Act (ESSA), also known as "Every Student Succeeds Act." This reauthorization made it compulsory that every Sates must establish rigorous standards for all discipline areas as well as for individual grade levels.

In 2001, President George W. Bush signed into law the No Child Left Behind Act (NCLB), which replaced Goals 2000 as the newest educational reform initiative. NCLB established a method of measurement as a stipulation for states to receive federal funding. While states are free to establish their own unique set of educational standards, the federal government mandates that states report math and reading scores for specific demographic subgroups who are considered disadvantaged. Within this new legislation are punitive directives for states failing to make adequate progress within these targeted subgroups. The new accountability measures within NCLB made it possible for there to finally be transparency in the educational system. It would now be possible to easily look at published reports that contain information on how student groups performed on standardized tests in a district or school campus. Before NCLB became the law of the land, scores of certain demographic subgroups not being served equitably by the system could be masked within schools, district, or state test averages. With the requirement of the new reporting guidelines, it was now possible to see yearly progress of these traditional underserved demographic subgroups.

Science Standards

In 1993, the National Research Council created the first nationally recognized set of science standards called the *National Science Education Standards* (NSES). It was from these new standards states created their own individualized standards in which they built their grade level courses. Within the NSES was the inclusion of an instructional methodology to be included with the standards themselves. As stated (NRC, 2000), Inquiry is closely related to scientific questioning, thereby forcing students to engage in inquiry using what they already know to gain additional information. While inquiry has been around since the early 1900s, it was this new set of standards that placed the learning of and about science front and center in terms of not just what students needed to know, but how it should be taught for students to acquire the skills of inquiry. Unfortunately, even with the inclusion of inquiry as an outcome and proposed method of instruction embedded within the standards, these standards alone were not able to change teacher behavior in the classroom as had been hoped. This is true even though the body of research clearly suggests that teaching through inquiry is effective (Flick, 1995; Delpit, 1995; Hurd, 1998; etc.).

In a broader context, standards help to define what and when to teach content, avoiding a curriculum catastrophe where everyone wants to teach units on penguins and butterflies. Standards provide a road map for instruction on which states can build course descriptions describing what will be taught and the expectations for what students will learn throughout a specific course. In this case, science standards are created to build on each other over time making sure the content to be learned is age appropriate.

As most may agree, the concept of content standards makes sense. Assessing an outcome of instruction also makes sense, especially at the teacher level. Assessments can be analyzed and used to improve future instruction. For example, if students are not answering a certain question correctly, the teacher can look at the question and how it is asked to make sure the instruction allows for students to be better prepared. Perhaps students seem to struggle with the concept of density. It is important to analyze the results of assessments to determine if the deficiency is in the actual concept of density or if it masks an underlying problem students have with fractions, especially denominators.

At a state level, it is also important to analyze standardized test data to determine where to focus attention for needs as well as look for practices that are working well. It is unfortunate that standards and outcome-based reforms have been misinterpreted as the evil mechanism used to punish students, teachers, and schools.

Conclusions

Teachers can take stock in knowing, standards are here and will not be going away anytime soon. Like most policies, they were put in place with the best of intentions, to look out for the needs of our most vulnerable groups. Unfortunately, the success has been mixed with regard to academic progress on individual disciplines. According to Dee and Jacob (2010), results indicate that NCLB helped increase achievement in mathematics in younger children, especially for disadvantaged students, particularly Hispanic students. Unfortunately, it had little effect on reading achievement. NCLB also encouraged schools to place an emphasis on mathematics and reading, while taking away the focus on science, social studies, and the arts (Koretz, 2008; Renter et al., 2006; Rothstein, Jacobsen, & Wilder, 2008).

Most would agree that a level of accountability is needed in any system, including education. But how that measure is used may be a contentious topic amongst the participants within the system (as well as those with oversight over the system). At the same time, it is vital the policy itself be reviewed to best maximize the effect of policy. Many of us have come to know the Peter Parker (AKA Spiderman) Principle, "With great power comes great responsibility. " It comes as little surprise that it may not be the tools of accountability that are problematic, but the implementation of such tools and as such may need to be kept in constant check.

References:

Bloom, B. S. (1969). Some theoretical issues relating to educational evaluation. In R. W. Tyler (Ed.), *Educational evaluation: new roles, new means*: the 63rd yearbook of the National Society for the Study of Education (part II) (Vol. 69(2), pp. 26-50). Chicago, IL: University of Chicago Press.

Dee and Jacob. (2010). The Impact of No Child Left Behind on Students, Teachers, and Schools, Brookings Papers on Economic Activity, Fall 2010. Accessed on 2/5/2022 @ https://www.brookings.edu/wp-content/uploads/2010/09/2010b_bpea_dee.pdf

Delpit, L. (1995). Other people's children: Cultural conflict in the classroom. New York: The New Press

Elmore, R.F., Ablemann, C.H., & Fuhrman, S.H. (1996). The new accountability in state education reform: from process to performance. In H.F. Ladd (Ed.), *Holding schools accountable: Performance-based reform in education*, 65-98. Washington, DC: Brookings Institution.

Every Student Succeeds Act, 20 U.S.C. § 6301 (2015). https://www.congress.gov/bill/114th-congress/senate-bill/1177

Flick, U. (1995) "Social Representations," in R. Harre, J. Smith, and L. v. Langenhove (eds.), Rethinking Psychology. London: SAGE. pp. 70-96.

Fuhrman, S.H. & Elmore, R.F. (2004). Introduction. In Susan H. Fuhrman and Richard F. Elmore, (Eds.). *Redesigning accountability systems for education*, 3-14. New York: Teachers College Press.

Hein, G.E., & Lee, S. (1999). *Assessment of Science Inquiry, in Inquiry: Thoughts, Views, and Strategies for the K-5 Classroom*, Washington DC: National Science Foundation, 1999.

Hurd, Paul. (1998). Linking Science Education to the Workplace. Journal of Science Education and Technology. 7. 329-335. 10.1023/A:1021871209239.

Koretz, Daniel. 2008. Measuring Up: What Educational Testing Really Tells Us. Harvard University Press.

National Research Council (2000). Inquiry and the National Science Education Standards: A Guide for Teaching and Learning. Washington, DC: The National Academies Press. https://doi.org/10.17226/9596.

Rentner, D.S., Scott, C. Kober, N. Chudowsky, N., Chudowsky, V., Joftus, S. & Zabala, D. (2006). *From the capital to the classroom: Year 4 of the No Child Left Behind Act*. Washington, DC: Center on Education Policy.

Rothstein, Richard, Rebecca Jacobsen, and Tamara Wilder. 2008. "Grading Education: Getting Accountability Right." New York: Teachers College Press.

Spady, W. (1994) Choosing outcomes of significance. Educational Leadership 51 (6), 18–22.

CHAPTER 17: VISUAL LITERACY

By Milt Huling, Ph.D. & Arlene Fonda-Korr, Ed.D.

The test scores have been reported. From the district office staff to the classroom teachers, this data is being scrutinized, as individuals try to understand each student's performance. In all examples, there is the desire to understand if the current instructional strategies are working to the benefit of the students. If the student's performance was considered inadequate, what was the reason for the inadequacy. Could it be that the nature of the dilemma was pedagogical? Perhaps a lack of understanding regarding the presentation of the inquiry-based instructional strategies was the causation for the problem. Many educators may even absolve the problem and declare it an issue created by the lack of reading ability of individual students. Thereby presenting poor reading skills as another conflicting contention.

The problematic nature of reading is an ongoing struggle in every classroom and is not confined to just science instruction. Research informs us that the magnitude of this issue is overwhelming, with only 35% of fourth graders reading at a level deemed proficient (NCES, 2020). The same research shows that the rapid increase in ELLs in the United States may be exacerbating the problem. According to the National Education Association, by the year 2025, 25% of public school students will be non-English speakers (NEA, 2021). The high number of students not reading on grade level combined with the rapidly growing number of students who are English Language Learners highlights the need to consider a unique instructional strategy for science. The authors propose that a focus on teaching visual literacy in science for those student populations mentioned should be considered.

In a previous article published in this journal (Huling & Fonda-Korr, 2020), the authors made their case for the "infusion of visual literacy into science instruction to promote academic achievement, both on assessments and the general learning of science concepts." Visual literacy is defined as the ability to interpret, negotiate, and make significance from information presented in this format. It is based on the notion that pictures can be "read" just as text and that meaning can be made through a process of reading the visual (Dur & Inanc, 2018). In concise terms, visual literacy is the ability to read, write, create, and make evidence-based decisions based on visual images. With this perception there has been a growing interest in the use of visual literacy strategies within the discipline of science, to reach all learners.

Imagine you are an ELL student, or a challenged reader who is considering taking a state science exam. A student with these challenges is presented with an exam question that is asking about the part of the plant involved with reproduction, for example. Although this is a fundamental question, if the student with reading difficulties is only using words, the question will present a real challenge. The student may recognize the term "Reproductive System," from previous explicit vocabulary instruction, but the answer choices may continue to be incomprehensible to the student.

But what if the question contained an image where more information could be derived, such as the example below?

Figure 1.

Parts of a Plant Diagram

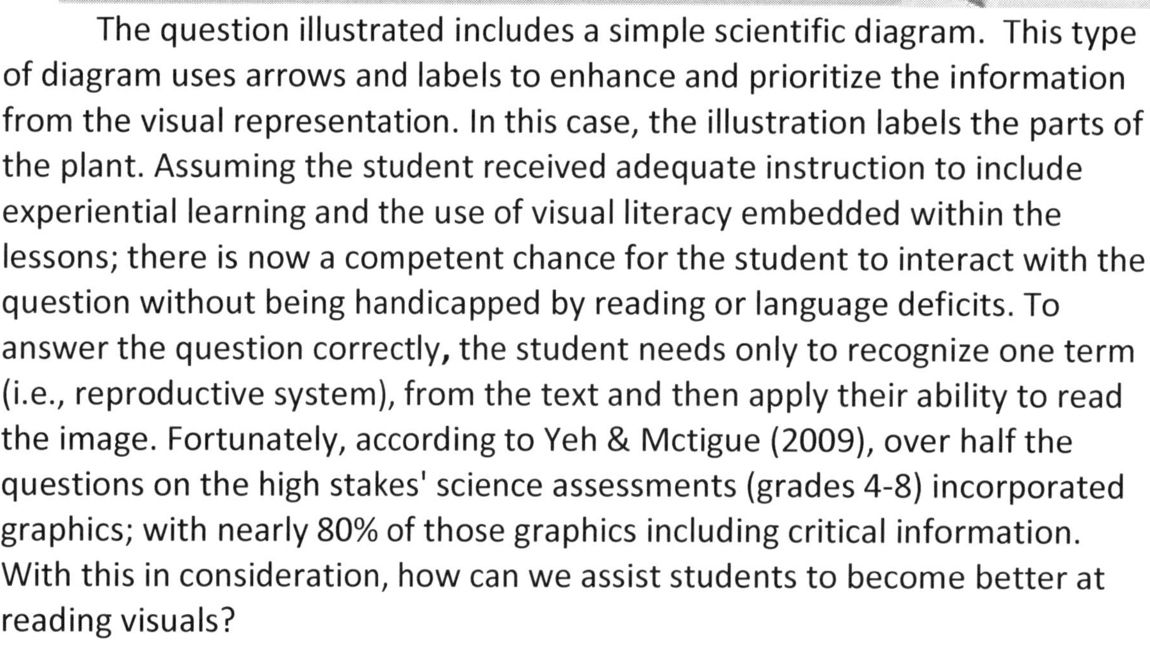

The question illustrated includes a simple scientific diagram. This type of diagram uses arrows and labels to enhance and prioritize the information from the visual representation. In this case, the illustration labels the parts of the plant. Assuming the student received adequate instruction to include experiential learning and the use of visual literacy embedded within the lessons; there is now a competent chance for the student to interact with the question without being handicapped by reading or language deficits. To answer the question correctly, the student needs only to recognize one term (i.e., reproductive system), from the text and then apply their ability to read the image. Fortunately, according to Yeh & Mctigue (2009), over half the questions on the high stakes' science assessments (grades 4-8) incorporated graphics; with nearly 80% of those graphics including critical information. With this in consideration, how can we assist students to become better at reading visuals?

Learning to read visuals is a skill ALL students must acquire. This instructional strategy is especially beneficial for those students who may otherwise struggle to read and comprehend the test in text format only. In the example below, you will see a strategy that has been utilized. The image shows a visual depiction of the Earth tilted on its axis. Will the student understand what is being asked by reading the text of the question? On the right of the Earth image is a series of questions we use when helping students learn to read visuals.

Figure 2.

Rotating Earth Diagram

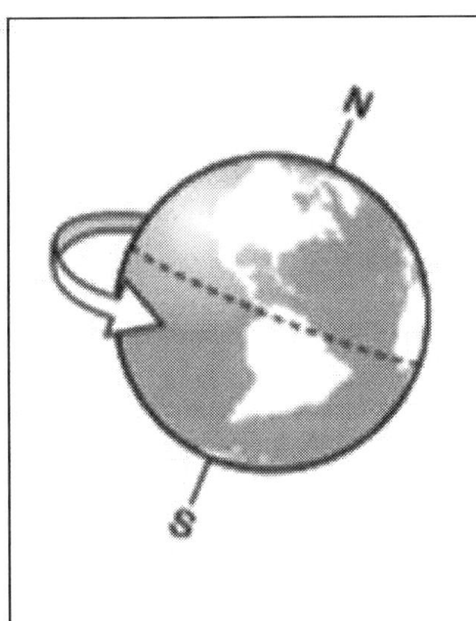

Ask:

- What do you observe?
- What can you infer about an image?
- What is the vocabulary connected with the image?
- What questions would you expect?

The first strategy the student may want to consider is to understand the components of the image. The figure includes a tilted axis marked by North and South poles. A student may assume an incorrect conclusion and presume the image is demonstrating seasons without noticing there is no sun or sun's rays shown in the image. The student may, also, observe that the image includes a large arrow showing a direction of motion. As it turns out, the large arrow has a critical purpose. Another step in better understanding the context of this image would be to consider familiar vocabulary that might be connected to this image. A student may recall the terms, "rotation and revolution," from previous explicit vocabulary instruction. In fact, these terms are cognates. Cognates are words in two languages that share a similar meaning, spelling, and pronunciation. When someone is learning a new language, a cognate is an easy word to remember because it looks and means the same thing as a word that you already know (Colorado, 2007).

For example, Biology in English means the same as Biología in Spanish. Based on Piaget's notion of mental schemata (Piaget, 1952), students' native languages are an additional resource as a learning tool to facilitate semantic learning. Checking to see if either of these terms are included in the question's text can also help the student decipher the question. The final step would be for the student to predict the type of question being asked. In this case, the answer choice would have to do with the phenomenon of day and night. Hopefully, the student will realize that the arrow is extremely important given its scale. In addition, the student's knowledge of cognates will guide the understanding that the question is asking about the rotation of the earth.

With the realization the arrow is extremely important given its scale, plus the included knowledge of cognates, the student will hopefully realize the question is asking about the impact of the rotation of the Earth. In this case, the answer choice would have to do with the phenomenon of day and night.

The research supports the importance of providing the struggling reader with access to visuals to enhance their understanding of science. For example, having the ability to read visuals is critical for ELL students categorized as "Entering stage/level," (WIDA, 2014). Nearly 60% of English words have Greek or Latin roots (Freeman and Freeman, 2014). How can we combine these research-based strategies into our visual literacy instructional practices to further aid our students to become academically successful? Research on second language acquisition and reading acquirement suggests that ELL students may transfer some language skills from their native language if the orthographies of the languages are similar.

The realm in which we now live has become more visual than ever before. We now exist in a visual age that reshapes how we communicate, perceive, and interpret the world around us (Barnard, 1998; Lester, 2000; Parsa, 2004; Sartori, 2004). As we scrutinize the important factors more closely, we observe the rapid change from page to screen and from print to image. Similarly, developing meaning from science text relies on understanding both the words and visuals of science (McTigue & Flowers, 2011). An important objective when planning a lesson is to provide instructional support such as graphs, charts, and diagrams to connect language and content. It seems prudent that for the students to gain a better understanding of science content, incorporating visual literacy strategies into our repertoire of instructional practices makes perfect sense.

References:

Allington, R.L., McGill-Franzen, A., Camilli, G., Williams, L., Graff, J., Zeig, J. (2010). Addressing summer reading setback among economically disadvantaged elementary students. *Reading Psychology*. 31(5), 411 -427

Barnard, M. (1998). Art, Design and Visual Culture: An Introduction. London: Macmillan

Blaut, J. and Stea, D. (1971). Studies of geographic learning. *Annals of the Association of American Geographers*, 61, 387-393.

Colorín Colorado. (2007). Using Cognates to Develop Comprehension in English, Retrieved April, 28 15, 2021, from http://www.colorincolorado.org/educators/background/cognates

Freeman, D. E. & Freeman, Y. S. (2014) Essential linguistics. Heinemann.

Huling, M. & Fonda-Korr, A. (2020). Visual Literacy: The Next Big Thing in Science Instruction: *Florida Association of Science Teachers Journal*. January 2021 (p.16-19)

Lester, P. M. (2000). Visual Communication: Images With Messages. Boston: Wadsworth Cengage Learning.

McTigue, Erin M., & Flowers, Amanda C. (2011). Science visual literacy: Learners' perceptions and Knowledge of Diagrams. *The Reading Teacher, 64(8),* 578-589.

National Education Association (2021). English Language Learners. National Education Association website retrieved March 21, 2021, from https://www.nea.org/resource-library/english-language-learners

National Center for Education Statistics. (n.d.-b). Digest of education statistics 2018, Table 204.20. Retrieved March 15, 2020, from https://nces.ed.gov/programs/digest/d18/tables/dt18_204.20.asp

National Center for Education Statistics. (n.d.). Digest of education statistics, Table 221.80. Retrieved March 15, 2020, from https://nces.ed.gov/programs/digest/d18/tables/dt18_221.80.asp?current=yes

Parsa, A. F. (2004). İmgenin Gücü ve Görsel Kültürün Yükselişi. N. Işık (Ed.), Medyada Yeni Yaklaşımlar. Konya: Eğitim Kitabevi Yayınları.

Piaget, J. (1952). Jean Piaget. In E. G. Boring, H. Werner, H. S. Langfeld, & R. M. Yerkes (Eds.), A History of Psychology in Autobiography, Vol. 4, pp. 237–256). Clark University Press

Sartori, G. (2004). Görmenin İktidarı: Homo Videns Gören İnsa. [Homo videns : la sociedad teledirigida]. (G. Batuş & B. Ulukan, Trans.) İstanbul: Karakutu

U.S. Department of Education, National Center for Education Statistics. English Learners in Public Schools (2017). Retrieved March 15, 2020, from https://nces.ed.gov/programs/coe/indicator_cgf.asp

Uyan Dur, Banu İnanç. (2018). The Relation Between Infographic and Visual Literacy. Conference Presentation: ITICAM 2018-4th International Trends and Issues in Communication & Media Conference, At Paris-France

WIDA's Board of Regents of the University of Wisconsin System (2014). 2012 Amplifications of English Language Development Standards. Kindergarten-Grade 12. Retrieved on 7/28/2021 from https://wida.wisc.edu/sites/default/files/resource/2012-ELD-Standards.pdf

Yeh, Y.Y., & McTigue, E.M. (2009). The frequency, variation, and function of graphical representations within standardized state science tests. School Science and Mathematics, 109(8), 435–449. doi:10.1111/j.1949-8594.2009.tb18291.x

CHAPTER 18: INTEGRATION OF MATH AND SCIENCE

By
Milt Huling, Ph.D. & Melissa Kelly, M.S.

According to NAEP (2019), the overall trend for science scores has remained mostly flat over the past decade. The same report contains a teacher survey revealing a lack of inquiry-based activities in science classrooms (NAEP, 2019). According to NAEP surveys of teachers (2019), only 18% of all fourth-grade students participated in inquiry-based practices. This trend worsens when disaggregated for low performing students as compared to their higher performing peers.

FIGURE 1. Percentage of fourth-grade students participating in inquiry-related activities (NAEP, 2019).

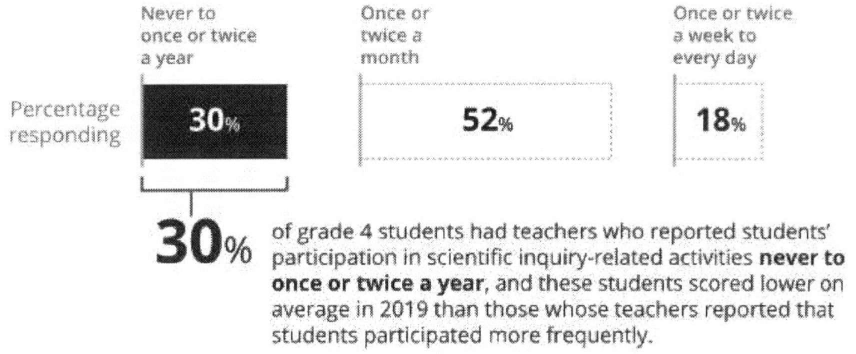

Unfortunately, it is all too often the case that science instruction plays second fiddle to other disciplines such as reading and math. It is also the case that even if time is provided for science by schools and districts, due to a lack of professional development, teachers may not have the knowledge or confidence in science further contributing to the lack of its instruction (Horizon Research 2013; McClure et al. 2017).

Like science, math scores have also been fairly stagnant given its preeminent focus, second only to readings hegemonic position within schools. Unlike science, mathematics is provided ample time in which inquiry-based activities can be performed. Surveys of teachers too provides interesting insight into the math world as compared to science. In 2019, only twenty-one percent of fourth-grade classrooms were reported as having a lack of adequate instructional materials and supplies. For an 8th grade classroom, this situation drops to nineteen percent cited by teachers as a limitation to adequate mathematics instruction.

FIGURE 2. Percentage of fourth and eighth grade students who lack adequate instructional materials and supplies.

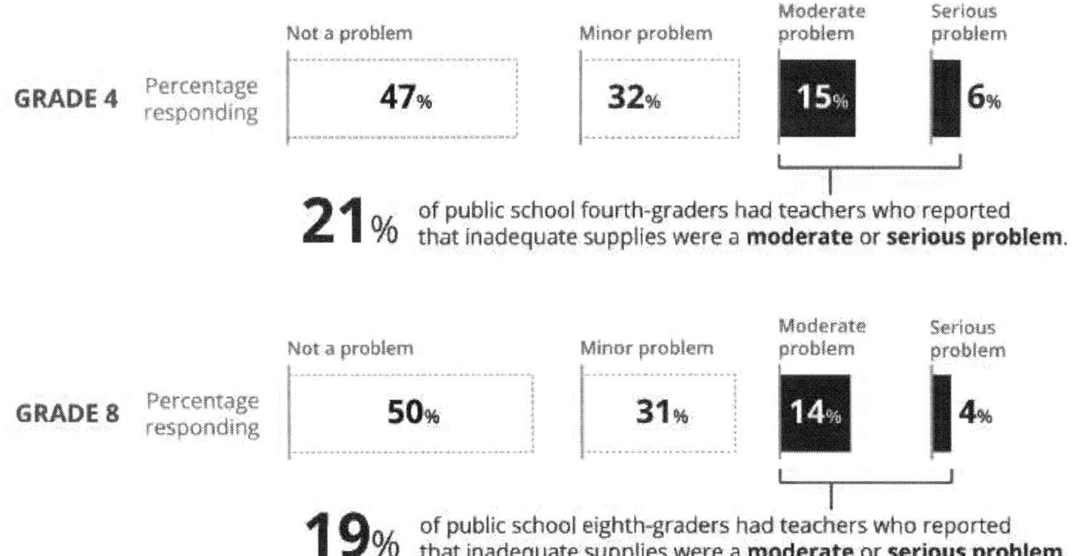

Defining Math and Science

Science can be thought of as a way of knowing. The creation of scientific knowledge involves a systematic study, through observation of experiment, of the structure and behavior of the physical and natural world. Mathematics can be defined as the logical "coding" system for the natural world. Mathematics provides a method to define the quality, structure, space, and changes in the natural world. In other words, mathematics provides the tools and language that can help to build understandings by revealing patterns, trends, and relationships in nature. Mathematics also provides a means of quantifying observations and providing a means to make predictions using mathematical models. It would seem obvious, given the commonalities between these two disciplines, that the integration of the two disciplines would be second nature, but why is it not common place in our classrooms? Could it be like many things in education the simplistic terms often used mask a more complex and multi-faceted meaning? In the next section, we will define the integration of mathematics and science, explain its importance in the classroom, and explore potential ways to easily integrate the two disciplines into classroom instruction.

Defining and Rationale for Integration

In a broad sense, integration is about the ability for teachers to use examples, data, and information from a variety of disciplines. This integration is to help students better understand key concepts, principles, generalizations, and theories in a specific discipline (Banks, 1993). It is the hope that when mathematics is integrated into science it provides students the ability to apply the discipline of mathematics in a way that is relevant and more engaging to a student. As well, students can come to understand that mathematics and science are interrelated.

While integration is critical to help students understand the important relationships, this does not mean integration is always necessary. At times mathematics can, and should, be taught separately from science for students to focus on learning a basic concept, skill, or procedure. In our rush to integrate, it is important to note that science and mathematics cannot always be an easy integration and a force fit may not be the best option. By assuming that integration is always needed we can easily miss the point of integration as a way of increasing understandings in both disciplines. As mentioned by Davidson, Miller, & Bethany (1995), "counting paramecia under a microscope generally does not constitute valid integration." There are times when it is best for both disciplines to stay separate enabling a more introductory focus on important concepts and processes before integration is applied.

Ways of Applying Integration

While there are multiple ways to integrate these two disciplines, the discussion here will be limited to the two most utilized. Perhaps the most common type of integration between math and science is that of *Process Integration*. For the novice of integration, it may also be the easiest to apply.

Process Integration is an approach where mathematics can be integrated into the inquiry process of science. Through the integration of mathematics into science, students, through experiences, can make a connection between the process of both science and math as they conduct experiments, collect, and analyze data, and report results.

An example of this type of integration can be common lessons used in elementary science classrooms utilizing ramps and marbles. One of these lesson types looks at the relationship of gravity and speed. In this lesson, a marble is rolled down a ramp and allowed to travel across a smooth surface for a defined distance. To collect data, students start a timer as the marble leaves the ramp and begins its travel across the smooth flat surface. The timer is stopped as the marble reaches the predetermined point. The students then use the data of time and distance to calculate speed. Data is organized in a table for different ramp heights (which serves as a proxy for gravitational force applied). The multiple trials at each ramp height are averaged. Data is then analyzed to examine the effects of the varying ramp heights to determine the relationship of ramp height to speed. A conclusion is drawn from this investigation and can be easily reported out to peers, thereby mirroring the process used by professional scientists.

Another commonly used method of integration is that of *content specific integration*. This type integrates instruction of both the disciplines of math and science and not just providing instruction in one while merely supporting the other. In the case of content specific integration, content is learned in both disciplines in a side-by-side manner. It should be noted that this type of integration involves more skill from the teacher as it requires the weaving together of two different concepts of the two disciplines.

An example of this type of integration involves the 3rd grade concepts of fractions and the transformation of energy. In the lesson, students are provided a sheet of chart paper, that they measure or fold to divide the paper into fractional parts (I.e., 1/4ths, 1/8ths, & 1/16ths). Horizontal lines are drawn on the paper to make observations easier. The chart paper is then taped to the wall so that the bottom edge rests on the floor. Students begin by dropping a tennis ball from a height of 1 (I.e., 4/4, 8/8, 16/16) and recording on a data collection sheet the initial drop height and the height the ball bounced back to. The difference in these two fractions is the amount of energy being transformed. Students continue collecting data as they drop the ball from decreasing heights, recording the return height, and finding the difference. Students are asked, what is the initial form of energy the ball has (answer: mechanical). Note: Potential and Kinetic energy are not used at this grade level, just the overall form of energy for motion, mechanical. Students are asked to identify the forms of energy the mechanical has been transformed into because of the ball's collision with the floor. With scaffolded questioning, students will arrive at heat and sound as the sources of energy.

By utilizing this integrated method, students are learning about the process of inquiry, transformation of energy, as well as honing their skills on the subtraction of fractions. This lesson can also be used as a 5th grade lesson by using two sheets of chart paper, one above the other, thereby extending the range beyond the value of one.

Conclusions

If we do what we have always done, then we will get the same results, a lot of math, very little science, and a lack of synergy between the two disciplines. By integrating math and science, the concepts of relevancy and applicability can become more prevalent through the student experience. All too often, science does not get as much instructional time as math in a typical class or school. However, science utilizes math during its minimal instructional time. Unfortunately, math does not often reciprocate by integrating science. Imagine if teachers stepped from their comfort zones and were then able to help students make real-world connections between the two disciplines of math and science. Instead of word problems in math, students could experience real-world connections. This integration would also provide subject matter equivalence and demonstrate how math and science can and should, go hand in hand.

References:

Banks, J. (1993). Multicultural education: Development, dimensions, and challenges. Phi Delta Kappan 75 (1) 22-28

Berlin, D. F. (1991). A bibliography of integrated science and mathematics teaching and learning literatu*re. School Science and Mathematics Association Topics for Teachers Series* (6). Columbus, OH: ERIC Clearinghouse for Science, Mathematics and Environmental Education

Berlin, D. F., & White, A.L. (1994). The Berlin-White integrated science and mathematics model. *School Science and Mathematics, 94*(1), 2-4

Davidson, D., Miller, K., & Bethany, K. (1995). What Does Integration of Science and Mathematics Really Mean? School Science and Mathematics, Volume 95(5). http://www.project2061.org/publications/designs/online/pdfs/reprints/8_davisn.pdf

NAEP (2019). NAEP Report Card: 2019 NAEP Science Assessment Highlighted results for the nation at grades 4, 8, and 12. Retrieved January, 24, 2021 @ https://www.nationsreportcard.gov/highlights/science/2019/

CHAPTER 19: WHY WRITING IN SCIENCE

There is overwhelming support within the science education community for a student-centered inquiry-focused science classroom (NRC, 1996, 2000; NGSS Lead States, 2013). Within this environment, students carry out hands-on activities, while teachers encourage peer-to-peer discussion and utilize strategic questioning techniques, but what about writing? Does time provided for science instruction, as compared to reading and math, preclude the inclusion of content writing. When was the last time your students completed a writing assignment within your science classroom? Just as speaking and listening helps students make sense of what they are learning and create connections with their daily lives, so too does writing. In other words, writing is thinking.

Rationale

Although there is widespread consensus as to the integral nature of writing as a component for learning (Champagne & Kouba, 1999; Hand et al., 1999; Kelly & Chen, 1999), is writing used as affectively as it could in the science classroom? Some teachers may assume the students are there to learn science, not learn to write. While true, this view ignores the benefits of having students write in the content area can bring. Other teachers may believe they are including writing as their students often record procedures, data, and conclusions in their science notebooks. Still others may have students write a summary to determine what they have learnt. In higher grades writing a lab report is a common strategy for including writing, but is this all students need? While learning to write like a scientist may be important for those students anticipating science as a career, writing can offer other benefits for the more casual observer of science. While all the previously mentioned methods of writing are important skills for a science student, writing in the content can offer many more academic advantages for the student. According to Judith Langer and Arthur Applebee (1987), writing in the science classroom can also help elicit prior knowledge, help to foster new learning, and consolidate and review ideas, and reformulate and extend knowledge (p.42).

One of the most important reasons for using writing in science is to foster conceptual understanding. Research conducted by Mason and Boscolo (2000) found that students who engaged in writing to reflect, reason, and compare, developed better understandings of content as compared to students having not experienced the integration of writing. As well, the inclusion of writing into science instruction improves students' ability to produce better arguments and had better outcomes regarding conceptual change (Fellows, 1994). Hand, Prain, and Yore (2001), cite how the utilization of 'writing to explain' provides more positive academic outcomes than students who only write to record or summarize. Therefore, it is vital that students must be engaged in, not just writing about science, but writing to learn science (Owens 2001). Writing to learn helps students build their knowledge through multiple ways, to include conjecture, explanation, comparison, and reformulation.

Writing to Learn versus Learning to Write

Unlike when teaching students to write, the writing to learn framework does not require teaching the process or revising a paper until approved by the teacher. Instead, writing to learn is a way to provide students with opportunities to recall, clarify, and question what they know and how they know it. In other words, writing to learn is a way for students to express their thinking through writing (Knipper & Duggan, 2006).

Within a classroom utilizing a writing to learn approach, a teacher models and provides examples for students. Many times, the teacher does so by becoming a participant in the writing experience. The goal is to allow students to make decisions about their own writing and even make mistakes in a setting of minimal risk. The goal of writing to learn is focused on increasing students' depth of knowledge of the content, not the process of writing, though improvements of writing skills may be a by-product (Hand, Prain, & Yore, 2001). Students may question why they must write. Simply put at some point all of us will need to communicate our ideas through writing.

Writing Across Grade Levels

Writing to learn can be used as a strategy to increase student achievement at all levels. For example, kindergarteners may write using pictures and then invented spelling as they develop language skills over time. In slightly higher grades (e.g., grade 1 & 2), concept maps can be used to improve scientific thinking by providing a meaning-making experience.

Concepts maps may even be utilized at higher grade levels when writing skills are more proficient.

What might be even more surprising about the effects of writing is that even ELLs can benefit from the writing to learn experience. According to Amaral, Garrison, and Klentschy (2002), ELLs not only benefit from a science experience that includes science inquiry and a plan to include writing, but after 4 years of this type of instruction can outperform their English-proficient peers on tests of writing and science. This research sends a strong message as the numbers of ELLs has increased in most areas of the country. It also provides strength to the argument to include writing to learn in conjunction with science inquiry for ALL students.

Why and How Do We Write in Science

It should come as little surprise that students are more likely and able to write when they have something interesting to write about. Within the inquiry-based science classroom, students spend time engaged in hands-on activities that can become an important part of their writing. Many times, within the science lessons, students record data, which can then be used within a writing to learn experience. Here, students make connections between the collected data and students' own lives thereby providing relevance to the lesson, which may otherwise seem abstract. A common writing prompt that is often used in science classrooms is to have students tell the story of a water molecule as it journeys through the water cycle. This process helps students make connections between places where water can be found on planet earth, states of matter, and the types of transformations (e.g., evaporation, precipitation, & condensation). Essentially, the writing assignment encourages students to create their own mental model of the water cycle.

The water cycle journey is an example of using students' own experiences and investigations to provide an opportunity for writing. A teacher's role would be to identify the potential writing prompts that relate to each lesson or concept. During the writing to learn experience, students will need scaffolding and support to be successful on writing tasks. Teachers must also model what they expect. Using the scenario of the water cycle journey, a teacher can share an example they wrote, or a student from a previous year, as an exemplar. Teachers must also keep in mind the purpose of writing to learn in the science classroom. At first, students should be allowed to use their everyday language to express their ideas, concentrating on ideas over spelling and grammar. By providing a low-stakes environment for writing, students are more free to experiment and explore the science content without the fear of failure or penalty as they complete their rough draft.

During the writing to learn experience, a teacher will provide feedback to help the student improve their writing by including more accurate scientific vocabulary. The teacher will also encourage students to provide more elaboration as a means of deepening their understandings of content. Feedback is critical for emerging writers, even though some teachers may struggle to move beyond the writing (i.e., spelling and grammar) toward one that lends itself to learning of content (Owens, 2001). A teacher must also guard against vocabulary that masks understandings. For example, while many schools require teachers to post the State standards being taught, if a student includes this statement, it does not mean they understand it. With the provision of ample feedback and support, learners will become not simply better writers, but better thinkers (Spandel & Stiggins, 1990).

Writing fluency is yet another reason students need to write often to help them make meaning of content. The idea is to get students to put their ideas down on paper quickly and accurately (Fearn & Farnan, 2001). This strategy can easily be accomplished using student science journals where they are expected to write about what they learned in brief timed events. For example, the teacher may ask students to write for 3 minutes at the beginning or end of class to explain what they learned. These interludes can help students commit ideas to memory, help make sense of what was learned and also provide information to the teacher about the quality of student knowledge and understandings of content. In other words, if students are not writing fluently, they may not be thinking fluently.

Conclusions

Education's current role for writing as an evidentiary expedition into a students' acquisition of knowledge is far from the goal of using writing as a learning tool. Student writing must advance beyond the replication and reproduction of science knowledge (Hand & Prain, 2006). This basis for writing as a learning tool is focused upon an interactive-constructivist approach and is essential if we expect increased academic achievement from our students (Yore et al., 2003). Unfortunately, the struggle to implement meaningful writing opportunities within the classroom has been underestimated and will need additional support in the way of pre-service and in-service training opportunities to change conceptions of science educators about the effectiveness of writing to learn (Rivard, 1994).

Though writing for many teachers is a culminating activity used to assess a student's knowledge at the end of instructional units, it is the authors' belief that writing should be placed front and center within the learning process, not just because of instruction. Students need opportunities to write often and in a low-risk environment. Students must be allowed to move beyond "the summary" if writing is to become part of the solution to improve students' reasoning ability and help them become critical thinkers about the information. To achieve this goal of transforming the writing in a science classroom is to take hold, then a concerted effort must be placed upon supporting this change by mobilizing the school administration, teachers, and other community-based stakeholders (Langer & Applebee, p 145).

References:

Amaral, O.M., L. Garrison, & M. Klentschy. 2002. Helping English learners increase achievement through inquiry-based science instruction. *Bilingual Research Journal* 26(2): 213–239.

Bybee, R. W. (1995). Achieving science literacy. Science Teacher, 62(7), 28–33.

Fellows, N.J. 1994. A window into thinking: Using student writing to understand conceptual change in science learning. *Journal of Research in Science Teaching* 31(9): 985–1001.

Ford, C., Yore, L. D., & Anthony, R. J. (1997). Reforms, visions, and standards: A cross-curricular view from elementary school perspective. Resources in Education (ERIC), ED 406168.

Halliday, M. A. K., & Martin, J. R. (1993). Writing science: Literacy and discursive power. Pittsburgh, PA: University of Pittsburgh Press.

Hand, B. & Prain, V. (2006). Moving from border crossing to convergence of perspectives in language and science literacy research and practice. *International Journal of Science Education Vol. 28,* Nos 2–3, 15 February 2006, pp. 101–107

Hand, B., V. Prain, & L. Yore. 2001. Sequential writing tasks' influence on science learning. In Writing as a learning tool: Integrating theory and practice, eds. P. Tynjala, L. Mason, and K. Lonka. Dordrecht, The Netherlands: Kluwer.

Holliday, W., Yore, L., & Alvermann, D. (1994). The reading-science learning-writing connection: Breakthroughs, barriers, and promises. Journal of Research in Science Teaching, 31, 877–893.

https://purdueglobalwriting.center/2011/05/21/writing-to-learn-vs-learning-to-write/

Institute for Inquiry (2022). Science Writing: A Tool for Learning Science and Developing Language. Exploratorium website. San Francisco, CA. Retrieved) 2/25/22 @ https://www.exploratorium.edu/education/ifi/inquiry-and-eld/educators-guide/science-writing

Knipper, K.J. & Duggan, T.J. (2006). Writing to learn across the curriculum: Tools for comprehension in content area classes. *International Reading Association, 462*–470. doi:10.1598/RT.59.5.5

Langer, J.A., & A.N. Applebee. 1987. How writing shapes thinking: A study of teaching and learning. Urbana, IL: National Council of Teachers of English.

Mason, L., & P. Boscolo. 2000. Writing and conceptual change: What changes? Instructional Science 28(3): 199–226.

National Research Council (2000). Inquiry and the National Science Education Standards: A Guide for Teaching and Learning. Washington, DC: *The National Academies Press*. https://doi.org/10.17226/9596.

NGSS Lead States (2013). Next Generation Science Standards: For States, By States. Washington, DC: *The National Academies Press*.

Norris, S. P., & Phillips, L. M. (2003). How literacy in its fundamental sense is central to scientific literacy. *Science Education*, 87, 224–240.

Osborne, R., & P. Freyberg. 1985. Learning in science: The implications of children's science. Portsmouth, NH: Heinemann.

Owens, C.V. 2001. Teachers' responses to science writing. Teaching and Learning: *The Journal of Natural Inquiry*. Summer: 22–35.

Patterson, E.W. 2001. Structuring the composition process in scientific writing. *International Journal of Science Education* 23(1): 1–16.

Saul, E. W. (2004b, November 17). Linking science and literacy in the science classroom. Keynote Address at a *National Science Foundation/National Science Teachers Association*-sponsored conference on Science Literacy, Seattle, WA.

Spandel, V., & R.J. Stiggins. 1990. *Creating writers: Linking assessment and writing instruction.* White Plains, NY: Longman.

Warwick, P., P. Stephenson, and J. Webster. 2003. Developing pupils' written expression of procedural understanding through the use of writing frames in science: Findings from a case study approach. *International Journal of Science Education* 25(2): 173–192.

Warwick, P., R.S. Linfield, and P. Stephenson.1999. A comparison of primary school pupils' ability to express procedural understanding in science through speech and writing. *International Journal of Science Education* 21(8): 823–838.

Yore, L. D., Bisanz, G. L., & Hand, B. M. (2003). Examining the literacy component of science literacy: 25 years of language and science research. *International Journal of Science Education, 25,* 689–725.

CHAPTER 20: TEACHING VOCABULARY IN SCIENCE?

By
Milt Huling, Ph.D. & Niqui Young-Pringle-Brown, M.S.

It is easy to see why teachers become frustrated when they hear two seemingly disparate sounding messages about the teaching of vocabulary. The discipline of science would seem to dismiss the front-loading of vocabulary while ELA suggests and supports the practice. This dichotomy of understanding and messaging in the realm of education is extremely interesting and equally troubling. Some would argue that the idea of teaching vocabulary explicitly (versus implicit vocabulary instruction) is not a dichotomy but instead vocabulary instruction along a continuum. And to some extent, it is a continuum; however, leading research points to explicit instruction – front loading in particular – is most beneficial for all learners. Is it really a different message between the two disciplines? Is the concept of front loading being miscommunicated? Or, is it merely a misunderstanding of the term, front-loading? Vocabulary is the cornerstone of basic to complex language skills, so it would stand to reason that vocabulary instruction should be at the forefront of classroom instruction across all facets.

Robust evidence suggests that students benefit from explicit vocabulary instruction. This instruction should span across the disciplines of not just language arts, but also science and social studies. By doing so, teachers support student with increased vocabulary, but also to better construct meaning from text (*Kamil, et al. 2008*). So, what is explicit vocabulary instruction? In short, it is vocabulary instruction that provides students with opportunities to actively engage with Tier-2 vocabulary words and the robust discussion associated with this method of instruction. This method of vocabulary instruction is tantamount in all disciplines because this contextual approach engages students and produces greater gains in vocabulary acquisition than the other methods of vocabulary instruction found in the classroom

What is Front-Loading?

What does front-loading vocabulary really mean, why is it done, and how is it accomplished? Wilhelm describes front-loading vocabulary as a way to assess, motivate, set purposes, prepare, protect, and support students. He proposes the following list as ways in which students are supported by front-loading of vocabulary and why it is important:

- To help students understand new content or concepts
- To help students use new procedures, strategies, and ways of doing things
- To promote generic knowledge about how particular text types are structured and make particular kinds of demands on readers.

Whether in literacy or science courses, clearly there is a need for students to know and understand the vocabulary before they are asked to apply it. This is especially true for ELL students where front-loading of vocabulary can help level the playing field, so to speak, and reduce student frustration (Echevarria, 2005; Lee, Penfield, & Maerten-Rivera, 2009). The idea of front-loading of vocabulary is further bolstered by the tenet that science concepts are best taught through an inquiry-based approach. Therefore, students must be exposed to this strategy of front-loading vocabulary. If front-loading vocabulary has been ignored, these students may experience some level of difficulty when attempting to engage in these scientific-based conversations. When students know the vocabulary, they are certainly better equipped to engage in these conversations and participate in the associated inquiry-based activities. By ignoring the power of front-loading vocabulary in the classroom, we are lessening the ability for students, especially our ELLs, to understand the concepts being taught.

Exposing students to difficult vocabulary before they encounter it in text form can be extremely beneficial, especially those words that may aid in initial comprehension or 'meaning-making' (Coffman, 2009). It has been found that students must have a working knowledge of 95% of the vocabulary in a passage in order to comprehend it (Lyon, 2009). For example, front loading in the ELA classroom would aid in student discussions about the terms “prejudice, bias, and bigotry" to create better connections with these terms before the reading of To Kill a Mockingbird. In the same way, disseminating the differences between data, evidence, observations, and inferences would benefit students before reading a science text involving the practice and nature of science (NOS). This skill of front loading is another way to scaffold learning through questioning and discussions and this then aids in familiarity with the vocabulary words. When front loading is equivalent to scaffolding, the result is that students make greater gains as teachers can gradually increase the complexity of the questions they ask of students as it pertains to vocabulary and the concepts associated with them. This skill is especially useful in science classes where terms are necessary to understand complex concepts.

While the terms used in the examples above play a critical role in the meaning-making of the text, some terms may play a lesser role. In such cases, a teacher may need to preview these terms so they do not encumber the student's navigation of the text. This factor is especially true in the science classroom. For example, in a science classroom, the text may include a reference to a scanning tunneling electron microscope. Elementary science students do not need to understand how they work or why the terms scanning-tunneling-electron are included in the microscope's name. What they may need to know is that a scanning-tunneling-electron microscope is an immensely powerful tool allowing scientists to make observations of really, really, small things, like atoms. All we have done is take this large complex word off the table. In this case, the complex term needs to be simplified to "take it off the table" so as to not obstruct the reading of the text. Those were a few descriptions of when and how a unit or lesson could start with some front-loading of vocabulary. In this way, frontloading takes on the role of making connections, teaching of structural analysis, and frontloading of information.

Oftentimes, teachers believe that best strategy for explicit vocabulary instruction is to create a separate lesson for a specific text and/or subject matter. Anderson and Nagy (1991) pointed out "there are precise words children may need to know in order to comprehend particular lessons or subject matter." As a result, teachers often feel the need to teach vocabulary in a silo – contrary to frontloading. A non-example of effective front-loading would be a separate vocabulary lesson disconnected from an immediate context where the words will be used. In those cases where this has been attempted, research shows that students tend to "mis learn" the words being taught (Brown, Collins, & DuGuid, 1989). Conlin, Powell, Daniel, & Elby add that improper front-loading of vocabulary may even disrupt the sense-making process (Conlin, D., Powell, K., Daniel, M. Elby, A., 2011).

Inquiry-based Science and Vocabulary

Science classrooms consist of complex terms, so it would stand to reason that the strategies employed for discussion and explaining why a phenomenon takes place often includes specialized vocabulary. Therefore, it would be a mistake to think there is no front-loading of vocabulary in the science classroom, but it is also true that frontloading may not look like a typical lesson in language arts that starts with the reading of a passage. While an inquiry-based lesson could start with a short reading passage, more often text exploration comes towards the latter part of the lesson. It is in this latter portion where students will be more active as readers and writers. This placement provides ample time for students to acquire vocabulary meaningfully within the context of the inquiry process. By doing so, the student acquires vocabulary before they are asked to apply it, thereby making the preceding instruction part of the front-loading process. Wilhelm, 2013 writes, "learning vocabulary is part of entering inquiry, doing inquiry, and entering into a discourse community." He argues that having knowledge discipline specific vocabulary is part of becoming scientifically literate in terms of speaking, listening, reading, and writing, but that doesn't mean vocabulary precedes a lesson. Olson, K. (2008) describes how science, or more specifically, scientists do not begin an investigation by matching vocabulary to the natural world. Instead, scientist begin their work with a question based in nature and uses vocabulary only to explain the rationale of the phenomenon to others. But how does this method help students learn and retain information? The idea of students learning vocabulary should be organic, allowing a student's development of vocabulary to be used to interpret and understand concepts versus simply memorizing terms.

Olson (2008) cites how students learn and retain information best when the process of learning starts with concrete representations of the science concept. Instruction should then move toward a more abstract representation and back again. This method allows the student to construct their own meanings of science terms as well as science concepts. Olson (2008) describes how this method incentivizes students to "earn the word" in the context of an inquiry-based lesson.

What may seem counterintuitive is that students can and do learn science concepts without the need for content specific language by using their experiences. For example, students may conduct an investigation on speed where objects speed up and slow down. Throughout the discussions those more simplistic terms are used as students construct an understanding of the phenomenon. At an appropriate time, a more specific vocabulary will be substituted into the discourse (i.e., acceleration). Students now have the context in which to make connections between a changing of speed and the new term, acceleration.

Accordingly, teachers can then elicit and leverage this new vocabulary over the course of instruction and beyond as the organic process of learning and thereby "earning the word." Within the science lesson, the teacher will start to use the appropriate vocabulary, prompting students to follow suit through written or oral discourse. Content-specific vocabulary may even be posted in the room either as an interactive word wall, or students may be prompted to connect the vocabulary to illustrations in their science notebooks as it is encountered within the lesson. As students do eventually encounter text, the process of acquiring more vocabulary will switch to the perhaps more familiar methods of using strategies of finding meanings such as: gist clues, synonyms, contrast, or author provided definitions or even making text connections.

What is the impact of having science being a support mechanism for the skill of reading? We are all reading teachers, a commonly heard statement, but is it true, and if so, what is the impact from learning science? Krashen (1976, 1981) describes the difference between the learning of a language (i.e., reading) via explicit instruction as opposed to the more naturalistic approach of acquiring a language via interactions with content, such as what occurs through science instruction. According to Gee, (1989, p. 21) "For learning the rules of a language, learners usually beat acquirers at talking about it, that is, at explication, analysis, and criticism" ... "... and acquirers usually beat learners at performance" (Gee, 1989, p. 21). It would seem both approaches are not mutually exclusive and, in some ways, reliant upon one another.

Strategies for Front-Loading

Anchor Texts

Frontloading is most advantageous when there is connection to a text and learning objectives within the domains of speaking, listening, reading, and writing. Keep in mind that frontloading is a strategy used to enhance a lesson. Certainly, this looks very different in the ELA classroom. For example, a teacher is covering a unit that aligns with the standards to assess theme, figurative language, foreshadowing, character and plot development, symbolism, and poetic prose. By using Sandra Cisneros' book, The House on Mango Street as an anchor text, the teacher can connect and compare this reading to other poetic prose and explicitly teach the assessed content by using the text. However, anchor texts in any content area promotes an integrated approach to learning and teaching.

Computer-Assisted Instruction

Frontloading can be enhanced with the use of technology – presentation software, such as PowerPoint, Prezi, etc.). Using a variety of contexts to connect pictures, words, and morphemes can be enriched with technology through pictures and sounds – a job for computer-assisted instruction. "Computer-assisted instruction and other techniques that use technology help student develop working memory skills and academic vocabulary by using a relevant and current medium" (Cuba, 2020).

Cognates

Using cognates and non-cognates when frontloading vocabulary can be especially beneficial to English Language Learners. Just think of the sheer number of science words that are derived from Latin and Greek roots. Frontloading vocabulary allows for the explicit instruction of words (pronunciation and definition) that can then be used to aid in instruction and comprehension.

All Together Now

In the ELA and science classrooms, teachers are able to use anchor texts to aid students in becoming more aware of cognates and providing strategies for how those cognates can be useful in the use of their native language to decipher English words. For English Language Learners, these strategies are powerful as they provide students with meaningful ways in which they can use transfer this knowledge about cognates to develop their knowledge in the language being used in the classroom. Explicit instruction by the teacher can then take place and can be further strengthened through the use of graphic organizers (visual cues supporting metacognition) This combination of strategies when frontloading helps students make the most of the skills they have already mastered.

Conclusions

For certain, teachers find it difficult to navigate the between often contradictory messages about vocabulary instruction. For science teachers we expect students to develop an understanding of concepts to help them better interact with the world in which they live. Teachers of literacy help students develop the skills to decode text using a myriad of tools. As citizens of the world steeped in science and technology, our students will one day need to make decisions based on information they gather from the media. It will be their skills learned through literacy along with their knowledge of how scientific knowledge is constructed that will help them become informed consumers of information. Shanahan (2015) reminds us that literacy transcends disciplines such as science and social studies. Though they are not the same, we cannot truly have one without the other. It is critical that a clear message be sent about two disciplines in terms of the front-loading of vocabulary. The key is to front-load appropriately to meet the needs of the students. In language arts, where reading may come at the beginning of a lesson, front-loading takes a more predominant place. This differs from science where inquiry takes the predominant role for the learning of content, it also plays a secondary role in the front-loading of vocabulary and providing opportunities or sense-making to occur. It is this change in vocabulary dominance that allows for the learning of science through inquiry to drive the learning of vocabulary, not the other way around, but one that always give way to front-loading.

References:

Anderson, R., and W. Nagy. 1991. Word meanings. In R. Barr, M. Kamil, P. Mosenthal, and P.D. Pearson, (Eds.), Handbook of Reading Research, Vol. 2, pp. 690–724. New York: Longman.

Brown, J. S., Collins, A., & Duguid, P. (1989). Situated cognition and the culture of learning. *Educational Researcher, 18*(1), 32-42.

Coffman, N. (2009, July). Multisensory teaching: Rescuing struggling readers at all grade levels. Session presented at the 2009 Summer Conference for the Alabama Branch of the International Dyslexia Association, Hoover, Alabama.

Conlin, D., Powell, K., Daniel, M. Elby, A., (2011). De-emphasizing science vocabulary with English language learners. A poster presentation on Saturday, June 4, at the 2011 meeting of the Jean Piaget Society in Berkeley, CA.

Cuba, M. J. (2020). Frontloading Academic Vocabulary for English Learners With Disabilities in an Integrated Classroom Setting. *Intervention in School and Clinic*, *55*(4), 230–237.

Gee, J. P. (1989). Literacy, Discourse, and Linguistics: Introduction. *Journal of Education*, *171*(1), 5–17. https://doi.org/10.1177/002205748917100101

Hammer, D. (1994). Epistemological beliefs in introductory physics. *Cognition and Instruction, 12*(2), 151-183.

Hofer, B., & Pintrich, P. (1997). The development of epistemological theories: Beliefs about knowledge and knowing and their relation to learning. *Review of Educational Research, 67*, 88-140.

Kamil, M. L., Borman, G. D., Dole, J., Kral, C. C., Salinger, T., and Torgesen, J. (2008). Improving adolescent literacy: Effective classroom and intervention practices: A Practice Guide (NCEE #2008-4027). Washington, DC: National Center for Education Evaluation and Regional Assistance, Institute of Education Sciences, U.S. Department of Education. Retrieved from http://ies.ed.gov/ncee/wwc.

Krashen, S. (1981) Second Language Acquisition and Second Language Learning. Oxford: Pergamon Press.

Krashen, S. and H. Seliger (1976) "The role of formal and informal linguistic environments in adult second language learning." International Journal of Psycholinguistics 3: 15-21.

Marzano, R., & Pickering, D. (2005). Building academic vocabulary: Teacher's manual. Alexandria, VA: Association for Supervision and Curriculum Development.

Miller, J. (2007). The impact of college science courses for non-science majors on adult science literacy. *A paper presented to a symposium titled "The Critical Role of College Science Courses for Non-Majors" at the annual meeting of the AAAS.* San Francisco.

Olson, J.K. (2008). Methods and Strategies: The Science Representation Continuum. *Science and Children, 46*(1), 52-55. Retrieved February 15, 2022, from https://www.learntechlib.org/p/101842/.

Settlage, J., Madsen, A., & Rustad, K. (2005). Inquiry Science, Sheltered Instruction, and English Language Learners: Conflicting Pedagogies in Highly Diverse Classrooms. *Issues in Teacher Education*, *14*(1), 19.

Shananhan, ??? (2015). Disciplinary Vocabulary, Shanahan on Literacy, The blog you sent me. Posted: 09 Jul 2015 10:45 AM PDT

Redish, E. F., Saul, J. M., & Steinberg, R. N. (1998). Student Expectations in Introductory Physics. American Journal of Physics, 66, 212-224.

Rosebery, A. S., Warren, B., & Conant, F. R. (1992). Appropriating scientific discourse: Findings from language minority classrooms. *Journal of the Learning Sciences*, *2*(1), 61–94.

Rosebery, A., & Warren, B. (Eds.) (2008). *Teaching science to English language learners.* Arlington: NSTA Press.

Swanborn M. S. L., & de Glopper, K. (1999). Incidental word learning while reading: A meta-analysis. *Review of Educational Research, 69*(3), 261–85.

Wilhem, J. (2013). The Question of Teaching Vocabulary: Which Words? In What Ways? *Voices from the Middle*, *2*(4)
http://missionliteracy.com/uploads/3/1/5/8/3158234/wilhelm_and_vocab.pdf

APPENDIX A

Lower Level Convergent: Adapted from McComas & Abraham (2004)	
Emphasis	Memorization, recall, rote drilling
Signal Phrases	Who, what, where, & when
Bloom's alignment	Knowledge level
Pros	Easy to develop questions and to anticipate student responses, so directing class discussion becomes routine. Helps identify students with large deficits in general knowledge.
Cons	Least effective method for enhancing knowledge transfer. Students who respond correctly may have memorized material but without understanding it.

Higher Level Convergent: Adapted from McComas & Abraham (2004)	
Emphasis	Reasoning and critical thinking which usually requires some direction from the instructor
Signal Phrases	Why, how and in what ways
Bloom's alignment	Comprehension and application levels
Pros	Helps students to make connections between facts and begin to understand relationships. Fosters critical thinking and skills such as compare and contrast.
Cons	Can lead to digressions in lesson plan, answers are longer and more elaborate and may not be easily anticipated by teacher.

Lower Level Divergent: Adapted from McComas & Abraham (2004)	
Emphasis	Synthesis of information and analysis of information to develop response.
Signal Phrases	How could..., What are some possible consequences..., Imagine...
Bloom's alignment	Analysis level
Pros	Focuses on critical thinking skills and allows for in-depth student discussions. May lead to more student-generated questions and conversations thus engaging the learner at a deeper level.
Cons	More difficult for teachers to determine in what direction the lesson might be drawn.

Higher Level Divergent: Adapted from McComas & Abraham (2004)	
Emphasis	Motivate students to higher levels of thinking and encourage creative thinking
Signal Phrases	Defend, Judge, Predict, If... then, Can you create, What is your opinion...
Bloom's alignment	Synthesis & Evaluation Levels
Pros	Stimulate knowledge-seeking and hypothesis generation.
Cons	Difficult and more energy intensive. Teacher must challenge his or her own way of thinking and encourage the learner to as well.

Made in United States
Orlando, FL
11 January 2023

28579702R00089